LB 2342 .S

P9-DIW-616

Sustaining financial support
for community colleges

New Directions for
Community Colleges

Arthur M. Cohen
EDITOR-IN-CHIEF

Florence B. Brawer
ASSOCIATE EDITOR

Carrie B. Kisker
MANAGING EDITOR

Sustaining
Financial Support
for Community
Colleges

Stephen G. Katsinas
James C. Palmer
EDITORS

SOUTH PLAINS COLLEGE LIBRARY

Number 132 • Winter 2005
Jossey-Bass
San Francisco

SUSTAINING FINANCIAL SUPPORT FOR COMMUNITY COLLEGES
Stephen G. Katsinas, James C. Palmer (eds.)
New Directions for Community Colleges, no. 132

Arthur M. Cohen, Editor-in-Chief
Florence B. Brawer, Associate Editor

Copyright © 2005 Wiley Periodicals, Inc., A Wiley Company. All rights reserved. No part of this publication may be reproduced, stored in a retrieval system, or transmitted in any form or by any means, electronic, mechanical, photocopying, recording, scanning, or otherwise, except as permitted under Sections 107 or 108 of the 1976 United States Copyright Act, without either the prior written permission of the Publisher or authorization through payment of the appropriate per-copy fee to the Copyright Clearance Center, 222 Rosewood Drive, Danvers, MA 01923, (978) 750-8400, fax (978) 646-8600. Requests to the Publisher for permission should be addressed to the Permissions Department, c/o John Wiley & Sons, Inc., 111 River St., Hoboken, NJ 07030; (201) 748-8789, fax (201) 748-6326, www.wiley.com/go/permissions.

NEW DIRECTIONS FOR COMMUNITY COLLEGES (ISSN 0194-3081, electronic ISSN 1536-0733) is part of The Jossey-Bass Higher and Adult Education Series and is published quarterly by Wiley Subscription Services, Inc., A Wiley Company, at Jossey-Bass, 989 Market Street, San Francisco, California 94103-1741. Periodicals Postage Paid at San Francisco, California, and at additional mailing offices. POSTMASTER: Send address changes to New Directions for Community Colleges, Jossey-Bass, 989 Market Street, San Francisco, California 94103-1741.

SUBSCRIPTIONS cost $80.00 for individuals and $180.00 for institutions, agencies, and libraries. Prices subject to change. See order form in back of book.

EDITORIAL CORRESPONDENCE should be sent to the Editor-in-Chief, Arthur M. Cohen, at the Graduate School of Education and Information Studies, University of California, Box 951521, Los Angeles, California 90095-1521. All manuscripts receive anonymous reviews by external referees.

New Directions for Community Colleges is indexed in Current Index to Journals in Education (ERIC).

Microfilm copies of issues and articles are available in 16mm and 35mm, as well as microfiche in 105mm, through University Microfilms Inc., 300 North Zeeb Road, Ann Arbor, Michigan 48106-1346.

CONTENTS

EDITORS' NOTES   1
Stephen G. Katsinas, James C. Palmer

1. Conflicting Interests in the Funding of the Early Two-Year   5
College
Robert Pedersen
Our understanding of public junior college funding prior to 1940 has
been strongly influenced by the ideology of current scholars. A close
reading of the historical record reveals that early junior colleges were
rarely subsidized by states, and often aggressively opposed by them.
Their costs were instead met by approximately equal contributions of
local tax revenue and unaided tuition. It can best be characterized as an
era of high tuition and low aid.

2. Increased Competition for Scarce State Dollars   19
Stephen G. Katsinas
This chapter describes the dramatically changed external landscape in
which community college leaders pursue state dollars and details how
other spending priorities in health care, K–12 education, and corrections negatively affect the states' ability to fund community colleges.

3. Seeking the Proper Balance Between Tuition, State Support,   33
and Local Revenues: An Economic Perspective
Richard M. Romano
This chapter argues that a relatively high tuition, high financial aid policy is the most equitable and efficient way to fund community college
operating budgets and promote access.

4. Leading the Fundraising Effort   43
G. Jeremiah Ryan, James C. Palmer
Community colleges now depend on fundraising to fill a growing gap
between institutional needs and financial support from tuition and
government taxes. As a result, fundraising has become a critical component of fiscal leadership. This chapter describes emerging ways in
which fundraising is being viewed and organized in the community
college.

5. Sustaining Financial Support Through Workforce 49
Development Grants and Contracts
Mary A. Brumbach
Workforce development grants and contracts are important methods
for sustaining financial support for community colleges. This chapter
details decision factors, college issues, possible pitfalls, and methods
for procuring and handling government contracts and grants for workforce training.

6. Caterpillar Inc.'s Think Big Program at Illinois Central College: 59
Sustaining Financial Support Through Collaborative Partnerships
John Stuart Erwin
This chapter describes the joint associate degree program between Illinois Central College and Caterpillar, Inc., and discusses how collaborative instructional programs can help sustain financial support for
community colleges.

7. Sustaining Local Tax Support for Community Colleges: 67
Recommendations for College Leaders
Michael Thomas Miller, Carleton R. Holt
Community colleges often rely on local taxes as an important revenue
source and must occasionally seek voter approval for a local mill levy
increase. This chapter describes strategies for planning and carrying out
a campaign for securing that approval.

8. Using Strategic Planning to Transform a Budgeting Process 77
Cary A. Israel, Brenda Kihl
This chapter describes a proactive, institutionwide budgeting process
that is directly tied to a community college district's strategic plan in
order to provide community college leaders with information they need
to make judgments about cutting or sustaining programs in difficult
economic times.

9. The Changing Role of the President as a Fiscal Leader 87
Daniel J. Phelan
This chapter examines challenges and options available to community
college presidents as their institutions increasingly rely on unstable
streams of revenue. Presidents, particularly those at institutions with
limited access to strong local tax support, require a new and expanded
set of fiscal leadership skills.

10. Literature on Fiscal Support for Community Colleges 99
James C. Palmer
This chapter reviews selected literature on the external fiscal environment in which community colleges operate and the ways community
colleges adapt to changes in that environment.

INDEX 107

EDITORS' NOTES

Since the 1970s, recurrent recessions and a burgeoning fiscal conservatism have forced community college leaders to live with fiscal uncertainty. Thirty years ago, Lombardi (1973) noted that the "golden era of community college financing peaked in the mid-sixties," as the public became more distrustful of social institutions and as access to education became a less urgent priority in light of other "local and national concerns . . . crowding education for first demand on public money" (p. 110). In words presaging the recession of the mid-1970s and the subsequent enactment of Proposition 13, which imposed limitations on property tax growth in California, he argued that the community college faced "its most serious crisis since the Great Depression" (p. 111).

This same concern is being voiced today, especially in light of beleaguered state budgets. In the wake of the 2001 recession, the November 2002 edition of the *Fiscal Survey of the States* noted that most of the states were in "fiscal crisis" because revenues were falling while expenses—particularly for health care—continued to rise (National Governors Association and the National Association of State Budget Officers, 2002, p. viii). And although the national economy has since improved, the July 2005 edition of the same publication noted that "most states still face tough budget challenges" (p. ix). The tenuous role of the state as fiscal guarantor can be seen in Table 1, which shows revenue streams to community colleges (except those operated as part of university systems) in 1980–81, 1990–91, and 2000–01 (the last year for which national data are available). Over the twenty-year period covered by this table, the proportion of funding accounted for by state appropriations declined from 48.3 to 34.8 percent, and colleges became more dependent on tuition and state and federal grants and contracts. Similar trends have been found in earlier analyses conducted by Merisotis and Wolanin (2000) and Watkins (2000).

As revenue sources shift and state appropriations become more uncertain, sustaining financial support requires an understanding of the external fiscal environment in which community colleges operate and constant adaptation by the colleges to changes in that environment. The chapters in this volume provide insights into both aspects of fiscal leadership. The first three chapters provide historical, political, and economic perspectives on the fiscal environment. In Chapter One, Robert Pedersen draws on the history of pre–World War II junior colleges to show how fiscal and political concerns, rather than ideology about student access, have been the driving forces behind decisions to raise tuition. The focus on fiscal and political trends

Table 1. Current Fund Revenues for Public Community Colleges (Excluding Those Operated in State University Systems), by Revenue Source, 1980–81, 1990–91, 2000–01

Revenue Type	1980–81 Revenues (000s)	Percent of Total	1990–91 Revenues (000s)	Percent of Total	2000–01 Revenues (000s)	Percent of Total	Twenty-Year Change in Percent of Total, by Source
Tuition and fees	1,006,170	14.5	2,865,200	16.9	5,920,371	18.0	3.4
State appropriations	3,344,986	48.3	6,857,749	40.4	11,482,438	34.8	–13.4
Local appropriations	1,207,662	17.4	2,893,270	17.0	5,050,019	15.3	–2.1
Federal grants or contracts	387,819	5.6	1,641,754	9.7	3,938,876	12.0	6.4
State grants or contracts	150,007	2.2	730,786	4.3	2,114,465	6.4	4.3
Auxiliary	432,955	6.2	1,029,433	6.1	1,671,026	5.1	–1.2
Other	397,955	5.7	957,976	5.6	2,771,169	8.4	2.7
Total	6,927,555	100.0	16,976,169	100.0	32,948,364	100.0	

Note: "Other" includes federal appropriations, local grants and contracts, private gifts, endowment income, sales and services of educational activities, hospital revenues, and income from independent operations. This analysis used imputed data.

Sources: IPEDS (Integrated Postsecondary Education Data System) and HEGIS (Higher Education General Information System) finance surveys FY1981, FY1991, and FY2001. Analysis by Billy C. Roessler, a doctoral candidate at the University of North Texas.

continues in Chapter Two, in which Stephen Katsinas describes the convergence of factors since the 1960s that have made state support of higher education more difficult to secure than in the past. Richard Romano then turns in Chapter Three to the economic principles of efficiency and equity, demonstrating their potential use in assessing the proper balance between tuition, state support, and local revenues.

The following four chapters describe internal institutional strategies used to sustain fiscal support in the face of uncertain state tax appropriations. In Chapter Four, Jeremiah Ryan and James Palmer suggest guidelines for the development of successful fundraising campaigns, and in Chapter Five, Mary Brumbach draws on her experience at Brookhaven College (Texas) to examine the management of restricted government contracts that have increasingly been used to subsidize workforce development. Chapter Six, by John Erwin, addresses the issue of corporate support for job training, and describes the joint efforts of Illinois Central College and Caterpillar, Inc. to train technicians for Caterpillar dealerships. In Chapter Seven, Michael Miller and Carleton Holt take on the issue of local tax support, drawing on the literature to examine approaches to securing voter approval for a mill levy increase.

Continuing with the theme of internal adaptation, the volume next turns to the role institutional leaders play in sustaining the fiscal viability of their colleges. In Chapter Eight, Cary Israel and Brenda Kihl describe the strategic planning approach implemented by the Collin County Community College District (Texas) to make hard decisions about fiscal priorities among the many competing demands that can be made on an institutional budget. Daniel Phelan then examines presidential leadership in Chapter Nine, and discusses the ways in which greater reliance on unstable revenue streams has required presidents to rethink their roles.

The volume concludes in Chapter Ten with James Palmer's review of recent publications dealing with fiscal support for community colleges. These writings include examinations of changing revenue streams to the colleges, descriptions of state funding mechanisms (such as performance-based funding) that attempt to base allocations on criteria other than enrollment, and analyses of how state fiscal support and regulations affect college autonomy. They also include descriptions of college approaches to sustaining fiscal support and making the most of the resources they have at hand.

Implicitly addressed throughout this volume is the question of how funding influences the community college mission. The ups and downs of public subsidies since Lombardi's 1973 analysis have led to recurrent discussions of the viability of the comprehensive curriculum and the need for colleges to carve out more defined market niches (see, for example, Bailey and Averianova, 1998; Levin, Perkins, and Clowes, 1992; Richardson and Leslie, 1980). In addition, reductions in government support for the colleges have led to reexaminations of open access—a pillar of the community college movement. For example, Vaughan (2003) calls for a redefinition of open access, arguing that although colleges can't afford to serve all *members* of society, they can take steps to serve all *segments* of society while at the same time limiting enrollments to levels that can be reasonably supported by institutional budgets. It is within this larger question of the funding-mission relationship that the chapters in this volume should be read. As always, success in sustaining fiscal support will hinge on college leaders' ability to articulate what that fiscal support is for.

References

Bailey, T. R., and Averianova, I. E. "Multiple Missions of Community Colleges: Conflicting or Complementary?" New York: Columbia University, Teacher's College, Community College Research Center, 1998. (ED 428 800)

Levin, B. H., Perkins, J. R., and Clowes, D. A. "Changing Times, Changing Mission?" Paper presented at the annual conference of the Southeastern Association for Community College Research, Orlando, Fla., Aug. 1992. (ED 361 056)

Lombardi, J. "Critical Decade for Community College Financing." In J. Lombardi (ed.), *Meeting the Financial Crisis.* New Directions for Community Colleges, no. 2. San Francisco: Jossey-Bass, 1973.

Merisotis, J. P., and Wolanin, T. R. *Community College Financing: Strategies and Challenges.* New Expeditions: Charting the Second Century of Community Colleges. Issues paper no. 5. Washington, D.C.: American Association of Community Colleges, 2000. (ED 439 737)

National Governors Association and the National Association of State Budget Officers. *Fiscal Survey of the States.* Washington, D.C.: National Governors Association and the National Association of State Budget Officers, Nov. 2002. http://www.nasbo.org/Publications/fiscalsurvey/nov2002fiscalsurvey-revisedFL.pdf. Accessed Dec. 15, 2004.

National Governors Association and the National Association of State Budget Officers. *Fiscal Survey of the States.* Washington, D.C.: National Governors Association and the National Association of State Budget Officers, July 2005. http://www.nasbo.org/Publications/fiscalsurvey/fsspring2005.pdf. Accessed Aug. 11, 2005.

Richardson, R. C., and Leslie, L. L. *The Impossible Dream? Financing Community College's Evolving Mission.* Washington, D.C.: American Association of Community and Junior Colleges, 1980. (ED 197 783)

Vaughan, G. B. "Redefining 'Open Access.'" *Chronicle of Higher Education,* 2003, 50(15), B24.

Watkins, T. G. "Public Community College Revenues, 1989–94." *Community College Journal of Research and Practice,* 2000, 24(2), 95–106.

Stephen G. Katsinas
James C. Palmer
Editors

STEPHEN G. KATSINAS *is director of the Education Policy Center at The University of Alabama.*

JAMES C. PALMER *is professor of educational administration and foundations at Illinois State University.*

1

Our understanding of the funding of public junior colleges prior to 1940 has been strongly influenced by the ideology of current scholars. A close reading of the historical record reveals that early junior colleges were rarely subsidized by states. Rather, their costs were met by approximately equal contributions of local tax revenue and unaided tuition, in an era that can best be characterized as one of high tuition and low aid.

Conflicting Interests in the Funding of the Early Two-Year College

Robert Pedersen

As the nation approaches the reauthorization of the Higher Education Act, the debate over who should pay for the college education of young people and those seeking vocational retraining will invariably be coated in rhetoric grounded in differing interpretations of historical practice. Some will argue for a policy of high tuition and low aid on the grounds that the benefits of an advanced education are largely private. Others will push for a policy of high tuition and high aid, believing that this nation—and particularly its two-year colleges—promotes access for America's disadvantaged through low costs to students. However, neither position accurately reflects the funding policy that governed two-year colleges prior to the late 1940s. In their infancy, public junior colleges were simply ignored by the federal government, whose principal concerns were land-grant institutions and historically black institutions such as Howard University. State governments actually opposed the establishment of public junior colleges, seeing them as a threat to scarce state revenues needed to expand emerging normal college systems. Only local governments, through their school districts, and families of near college-age youth found reason to invest in these institutions. For the one, the benefit of a public junior college was as a reflection of "boosterism," or community pride. For the other, a local college, whatever its "grade," allowed parents to maintain supervision of their impressionable children for an additional two years before they would be faced with navigating the "moral rapids" that was the typical state university. Self-interest dictated funding decisions, then as now.

Any discussion of the history of community college funding begins with the fact that, in contrast to other sectors of higher education, they are exclusively public institutions. For this reason, community college leaders and scholars should view funding through the discipline of public policy. This perspective informs such basic issues as how the funding of these institutions evolved, to what end they were funded and should be funded into the future, and the manner of their past and future funding. This forms the central argument of this chapter. From the institution's outset, and well into the second half of the twentieth century, advocates of two-year colleges were forced to compete with other public entities for state support. Local two-year college proponents often came into conflict with their state legislature over the allowable amount of tax-based support that could be taken— even from local sources—and such conflicts were the primary determinant of community college funding policy throughout the first half of the twentieth century.

Although education historians generally agree with the public policy perspective, they are nevertheless sharply divided as to the underlying intent of the policy that guided funding of public junior colleges before 1940 and that continues to influence that funding into the twenty-first century. One camp of historians, known as the *advocates,* holds that two-year colleges have been, from their beginning, either free or extremely low cost, relying on a mix of local property tax revenue and state aid to further their role in promoting universal access to higher education. As Michael Brick (1963) observed, these institutions arose from the "soil of America's cultural, economic, and political heritage" (p. 3). Brick's junior college was born of America's Jacksonian belief in individual worth, its acceptance of social mobility, its encouragement of technological innovation, and its willingness to invest in human capital development. For the advocates, public two-year colleges were and are a *pure good,* and for this reason entitled to full public funding.

For the other faction, most often referred to as the *critics,* the community college is also described as a low-tuition institution, but it is funded from the public purse to advance very different policy ends. As initially argued by Hansen and Weisbrod (1969), the state aid appropriated on a per-student basis to such flagship institutions as the University of California represented an intentional and substantial subsidy of the generally affluent students who attend major state universities. In contrast, the far lower per-student appropriations granted by legislatures to two-year colleges are intended to lessen the benefit of a higher education for the largely middle- and lower-class students who have been diverted to community colleges because of their economic status. The critics contend that, as a matter of public policy, unequal public subsidies in higher education were intentional, and intended to restrict intergenerational social mobility.

The community college's critics further hold that this policy of inequitable funding among the sectors of public higher education is not of recent vintage. Brint and Karabel (1989), for example, trace the origins of this policy to decisions made in the 1920s and 1930s. They claim that public two-year colleges of this era purposefully maintained a policy of relatively low tuition as an integral part of a strategy to induce economically and socially marginal students into a sector of postsecondary education whose curricula were heavily weighted in favor of low-status, terminal vocational programs. In their view, "Tuition charges [at junior colleges] were low or non-existent at a time when most families could not afford to send their children away, even to the relatively inexpensive public universities" (p. 54).

What the Historical Record Reveals

A fundamental flaw in the interpretations of both advocates and critics of early junior college funding policy is that neither view is supported by the historical record. With the exception of California, whose two-year colleges benefited from a onetime windfall of federal funds (Joyal, 1932), from 1904 until the late 1940s junior colleges in virtually every other state divided the cost of instruction between a local property tax levy and a substantial student tuition. At a time when, according to Prall's estimate (1930), a student's total cost of instruction approximated $300 a year, junior college students generally paid somewhere between $100 and $150 per year in tuition.

This is not to suggest that the two-year college's early advocates concurred with a reliance on tuition income as a major source of continuing institutional funding. Rather, as the record reveals, in virtually every state that maintained a junior college before 1940, any consideration of equity or access was trumped by local taxpayer interest in moderating the impact of a junior college on the local school levy, necessitating increases in student fees and tuition. For example, Goshen, Indiana's "six-year high school" opened in 1904 with a tuition of $30 a year—a substantial sum at a time when white-collar workers earned less than $1,000 a year and there were as yet no systematic programs of financial aid (Hedgepeth, 1905). Moreover, the school's superintendent, Victor Hedgepeth, did not argue in favor of tuition on anything approaching ideological or policy grounds. Rather, even though he acknowledged that tuition was likely illegal in a pubic high school, he felt that it would help "mature" those attending the school's junior college program if they were required to pay a meaningful portion of its cost, much as if they were attending a private college.

Admittedly, the junior college's national proponents strongly and consistently objected to the use of tuition to offset public support of the institution. To quote Prall (1930), "A junior college cannot be expected to be self-supporting" and still provide access to young men and women of limited means (p. 20). And Prall was not alone. One of the nation's leading junior college proponents—the University of Minnesota's Leonard Koos—strongly criticized public junior colleges for levying substantial tuition charges as a means of meeting their basic instructional costs. Anything beyond the most nominal of tuition charges, Koos (1924) contended, would undermine the national policy of greater educational efficiency that was

Table 1.1. Resident Tuition and Fee Charges, Selected State Universities and Junior Colleges, 1928

Arizona	University of Arizona	$30
	Phoenix Junior College	$60
Iowa	University of Iowa	$90
	Burlington Junior College	$100
	Mason City Junior College	$60
	Sheldon Junior College	$105
Oklahoma	University of Oklahoma	Free
	Okmulgee Junior College	$125
	McAlaster Junior College	$200
Texas	University of Texas	$30
	Brownsville Junior College	$152
	South Park Junior College	$145
	Temple Junior College	$200

Source: Hurt, 1928.

prompting the "inevitable reorganization in secondary and higher education" implicit in the emergence of the junior college (p. 620). For Koos, "Any policy should be followed which is unlikely to oblige the communities maintaining [a junior college] to levy a tuition charge" (p. 620). Such was the only proper policy, according to Prall (1930), for the newest sector of "the free, public school" (p. 18).

Unfortunately for those with limited access to higher education, and despite the arguments of Koos, Prall, and other national figures in the early junior college movement, substantial tuition and fees were by far the norm at public two-year colleges of the era. A 1934 survey of 150 public junior colleges conducted by the U.S. Bureau of Education found that nearly two-thirds charged tuition, and most of those that did not were in California (Greenleaf, 1934). Oklahoma's junior colleges were more the norm. As Cotton (1929) reported, of Oklahoma's twenty-six junior colleges, only two—those sponsored by Muskogee and Ponca City—were tuition-free, and then only for local residents. Although California may not have followed this trend, according to Hurt (1928) the cost of attendance at a junior college in many states was substantially greater than tuition at the proximate state university, as reflected in Table 1.1.

The Historian's Reaction

For a historian, the first question posed by the advocates' and critics' mutually exclusive analyses of tuition and its relationship to the purposes of the open-access community college is whether primary source evidence supports either position, or suggests yet a third interpretation. Were the tuition charges levied at most two-year colleges during the first half of the twentieth century the result of conscious policy, or were they a response to conflicting interests based on changing and objective economic and political conditions? Was the decision of local school boards to charge students a substantial tuition the reflection of ideology or of entirely pragmatic, nonideological factors? As is documented throughout the following sections, early public junior colleges were neither the beneficiaries of some Jacksonian ideology nor the victims of class conspiracy when it came to their funding. The sources and levels of contribution were, as will be shown, determined by the nonideological, self-interested agendas of those factions—largely aspiring communities and conservative parents—who directly benefited from their local community college.

A second consideration facing the historian is what weight to give California events in the overall history of the public junior college. Among historians of the two-year college, California is routinely ascribed a special importance in providing the impetus to the establishment of junior colleges across the nation (Lange, 1916; Levine, 1986; Proctor, 1927). What this common presumption overlooks—with respect to funding in general and tuition in particular—is that California was the beneficiary of an unprecedented windfall from a onetime federal payment for certain oil and mineral leases. With the encouragement of Will C. Wood, its secondary education commissioner, the California legislature appropriated these revenues to create the first permanent junior college fund that would provide an exceptional level of state aid to those communities that organized junior college districts in conformity with the state's highly proscriptive Junior College Act of 1921. To qualify for payments from this fund, a proposed junior college district was required to have a minimum property assessment of $10 million, essentially ruling out the type of small, rural communities that established junior colleges throughout Iowa, Oklahoma, and other parts of the Midwest. Moreover, those California districts seeking aid under the 1921 act had to first secure the endorsement of the state board of education and then win voter approval through a special referendum. But most importantly, those junior colleges that drew upon California's fund were not required to shift resources away from their elementary and secondary schools—which was, without question, the single greatest source of opposition to the junior college in the Midwest. In short, California was far more the exception than a model, and the history of its two-year college funding, as exceptionally well described by Joyal (1932), is best set aside for separate treatment. To better understand the policy context that shaped funding of the pre-1940 junior college, one should look to those states, such as Iowa, Oklahoma, Texas, and Kansas, in which these schools flourished but state support was absent.

State Interests: The Obstacle to a Tuition-Free Junior College

As anyone directly familiar with the state legislative process will attest, a pragmatic self-interest, rather than ideology, shapes the actions of state legislatures. Legislative sessions are too brief and infrequent to enable legislative factions to achieve overtly ideological ends, and legislatures are bound by strict constitutional constraints that make the pursuit of expressly ideological ends, irrespective of cost, virtually impossible. Beyond their challenging constitutional responsibility to adopt bills to fund basic services and elementary and secondary education, legislatures must, in forty-nine of the fifty states, also adopt a balanced operating budget. These two requirements alone prompt state legislators to resist any addition to the institutions receiving recurring state appropriations, for such an expansion only results in an additional claimant on already scarce state resources. Interest groups—from the disabled and dislocated workers to preschools and community colleges—may pursue the security of a line item in a state budget, but the legislative barriers to this goal are necessarily considerable, so that few petitioners succeed in achieving this objective no matter the soundness of their policy arguments.

Securing State Recognition. Even if proponents of two-year colleges have the general support of legislators, it is not a simple process to translate such support into a meaningful level of state aid. A first and necessary condition to such funding is an institution's recognition in state law. In a number of states—Utah, Louisiana, Washington, and Ohio—this fundamental principle of state constitutional law served as an effective deterrent to the organization of two-year colleges into the 1940s. In these states, legislators were not the only ones concerned about the potential impact of junior colleges on the resources that would be available to already established sectors of education; state school superintendents also feared that money allocated to elementary and secondary education might be diverted by "aspiring" communities to their junior colleges (Foote, 1928).

It was specifically this lack of recognition (or, in legal terms, "definition") that provided the constitutional basis for Ohio attorney general Edward Turner's successful prohibition of public junior colleges in his state despite widespread local interest (Turner, 1928). But, reflective of an era when local communities still provided close to 90 percent of the funding for their schools, rulings like Turner's were as often ignored as adhered to by school districts. This was the case in Illinois, where that state's attorney general ordered the suspension of Joliet Junior College and other junior colleges there, only to find that his order was simply ignored (Hardin, 1975). Although state attorneys general and governors may have had the law, state interests, and policy firmly on their side, in contrast to the situation in the early twenty-first century they often found that they lacked the necessary leverage to enforce their will on those school districts that simply chose to exceed the limits of their legal authority.

State Opposition to Junior Colleges. Well before 1910, a small number of progressive high schools had embarked on a variety of locally inspired and funded curricular initiatives—known as everything from "upward extension programs" and "six-year high schools" to "university extension centers" and even "postgraduate programs"—to test the upward limits of the public high school's curriculum. This was not, as suggested by Veysey (1965), a period of consolidation in American education but rather one of remarkable experimentation. At no other time in American history would a public school system, as was the case in Detroit, place a medical college and normal school under its authority, or as happened in Newark, New Jersey, seek to use a junior college as the linchpin of a truly comprehensive public school system that would include a law school and a college of pharmacy.

By 1917, the extent of such extralegal curricular experimentation by the public schools had reached a point where state governments found themselves increasingly hard-pressed to ignore these initiatives if they were to preserve their constitutionally mandated oversight of public education. In that year, four states—Kansas, Michigan, Missouri, and California—adopted the first legislation to define junior colleges in state law and permit local districts to establish and spend public funds on these colleges. Obviously, the proponents of the junior college might well see this first wave of legislation to extend legal recognition to the junior college as a significant advance. But a closer reading of these laws makes clear that the real intent of those adopted by Kansas, Michigan, and Missouri was to discourage communities from overextending their local revenues in order to join the "college crowd" when many had yet to fund their elementary and secondary schools fully and adequately. These acts required, for example, that any school board wishing to establish a junior college must first secure the approval of the state board of education. Further, the authority to establish a junior college, which had previously rested with school boards alone, was transferred to local voters, who were required to approve a junior college through a special referendum. But most importantly, none of these statutes authorized what communities most wanted—state aid to offset some of the cost of a junior college.

Although some states chose to address the "problem" of the junior college before 1930 through legislation, other states opted for different strategies to accomplish the same end. For example, in Ohio local interest in the junior college had developed early, primarily among the state's western communities that had been bypassed by the wave of nineteenth-century private college foundings, and, the Ohio State University's W. W. Charters (1929) observed, by parents who believed their children were simply too young to survive the moral temptations of a large university campus. Further fueling interest in the junior college was a committee report of the

Ohio College Association in which its chair, George Zook (1928), advocated a state system of junior colleges. Faced with the prospect of school districts acting on their own initiative, as had happened in Illinois and Iowa, and concerned that elementary and secondary schools would be shortchanged as school districts sought to meet the expenses of a junior college, Edward Turner, state attorney general, issued his 1928 opinion specifically denying Ohio's school districts the authority to sponsor a junior college under any circumstance, even if wholly supported by student tuition. Turner (1928) noted that the term *junior college* was nowhere defined in Ohio law and therefore could not designate a class of schools eligible for any form of public support. Further, although not denying the state legislature the right to authorize a variety of higher institutions, such as the municipal colleges at Cincinnati and Toledo, he determined that the legislature had not extended a comparable right to local school boards. As any authority exercised by a school district must first be "clearly and distinctly granted" in statute, Turner concluded that no local public junior college could be established or operated in Ohio. The Ohio legislature sided with Turner and against Zook and his committee, refusing to adopt permissive legislation. No school district proved willing to challenge Turner.

Of all the states, likely the most extreme example of state governmental opposition to locally funded junior colleges can be found in the state of Washington. As was the case in California, the state university was located at some distance from such developing population centers as Centralia and Yakima Valley. Unable to secure either a state or private college, each of five Washington communities opted instead to establish a public junior college as the best remaining option to provide their communities with proximate higher education. At the same time, aware of the tenuous legal standing of junior colleges, these communities appropriately sought legislative authorization—and failed in their quest for some twenty-five years. Unfortunately for these school districts, during this quarter-century politics in Washington State was dominated by its exceptionally conservative governor, Roland Hartley, who freely and frequently used his veto power to block junior college legislation.

According to state records, bills modeled on California's 1921 Junior College Act were introduced and struck down in every session of the Washington legislature from 1927 through 1939. In 1929, for example, a broad-based coalition of schoolmen, local boosters, and others came closest to victory with the introduction of HR 195. Although facing only token opposition in the legislature, HR 195 was, according to form, promptly vetoed by Governor Hartley. In his veto message, Hartley characterized his state's expenditures on education as "excessive" and decried the seemingly endless "pyramiding of educational functions." As he bluntly stated, "The way to reduce taxes is to quit spending the people's money" (*Senate Journal of the Twenty-First Legislature,* 1929, n.p.).

Interestingly, during this period of legislative struggle those Washington communities that sponsored a junior college did not abandon their institutions. Rather, they countered with a variety of strategies to fund their colleges adequately until Hartley's opposition could be overcome. In 1927, for example, Centralia and the other communities with junior colleges converted them into "quasi-public" institutions. The junior colleges were reorganized under independent governing boards and these boards then contracted with their communities' school districts for needed services, paid for by a mix of student fees, donations, and business subventions—promissory notes that guaranteed sufficient revenue should tuition and donations fail to meet a junior college's cost.

Opposition from State Universities. A second, if less serious, source of opposition to the public junior college originated in a number of state universities, and this opposition often proved sufficient to block the adoption of enabling junior college legislation ("The Junior College Movement," 1927, p. 171). For example, in Wyoming during the 1920s and early 1930s several small cities expressed an interest in establishing a junior college (*Wyoming Community College Records Manual,* n.d.). With its only public university located in the far southeastern corner of the state, the challenge to access presented by geography was particularly influential in fostering local interest among the state's widely dispersed towns in securing some form of proximate higher education. As Karl Winchell (1931) reported, many of the state's larger high schools had already begun to offer a limited number of postgraduate courses, for which the University of Wyoming had decided to grant credit. Further, according to Winchell, the maintenance of junior colleges would not impose an undue hardship on the taxpayers of Wyoming's larger communities. As he calculated, at least five Wyoming communities had the necessary tax base to support a credible junior college program. It was his judgment that any obstacle to the organization of junior colleges in Wyoming came from without, and not from within, the state's communities.

Subsequent events confirm Winchell's assessment of the obstacles faced by junior college proponents in Wyoming. Throughout the 1930s, the Wyoming legislature adamantly opposed the adoption of legislation enabling junior colleges, rejecting bills in three successive sessions: 1933, 1935, and 1937. Civic leaders in Casper, Rock Springs, and Sheridan simply could not overcome the range of interests allied against these bills. As Robert Lahti (1961) suggested, legislative opposition to locally funded junior colleges prevailed through the alliance of two primary factions. First were those legislators who believed that the state should not permit a school district to divert tax revenue in support of a junior college until adequate provision had been made for its grammar and high schools—a mark few Wyoming school districts could honestly claim to have met. The second faction consisted of legislators who held that public junior colleges were simply not needed in Wyoming, despite the great distances and challenging geography that isolated the University of Wyoming from every one of the state's larger communities except Cheyenne. For this faction, the adoption of permissive junior college legislation was not in itself so much a concern as would be the potentially negative impact of a growing number of junior colleges on a seriously underenrolled state university; as late as 1935 the university had only slightly more than fifteen hundred students. For the legislature to allow such towns as Casper, Rock Springs, and Sheridan to sponsor a junior college was to virtually ensure an enrollment decline at the university and a proportionate decrease in revenues needed to meet the fixed costs of its dormitories and other facilities.

State and Local Interests Clash to Set Funding Policies. As George Zook (1922) discovered, and Leonard Koos (1924) echoed, taxpayers in such communities as Kansas City, Missouri, Grand Rapids, Michigan, and Joliet, Illinois, came to question the equity of legislative policy that required them to bear a substantial share of the growing costs of their junior colleges when the expenses associated with students at state colleges and universities were uniformly distributed over all state taxpayers. In pursuit of greater tax equity, one option open to these communities was to charge a relatively substantial tuition to offset costs that otherwise would have been levied against the local tax base. Because only a relatively small proportion of youth earned a high school diploma (at the time, a prerequisite to junior college admission), there was a strong equity argument that the relatively few high school graduates eligible to enroll in a junior college should bear a cost at least equal to the private benefit they enjoyed by not having to relocate to a distant state college or university. This rationale is implicit in the legislation that authorized junior colleges in Nebraska and Iowa. Based on a widely accepted standard of $200 to $300 in annual per-student instructional costs, the Nebraska legislature required that any public junior college would charge an annual tuition of $108. In the Junior College Act of 1927, Iowa's legislature set tuition for its junior colleges at "the full cost of instruction." Because the Iowa legislation failed to stipulate how this cost was to be determined there was considerable variance in tuition charges among the state's junior colleges, but in all cases it was substantially more than the charges at Iowa's two state universities (see again Table 1.1).

In time, communities came to recognize the basic inequity of state-mandated funding schemes that imposed the cost of a junior college education on students alone (as in Iowa) or on a mix of students and sponsoring communities. As long as total junior college enrollments remained low (and the typical junior college of this period had fewer than two hundred students) this inequity could continue, because those who chose to attend their local junior college did so for reasons other than cost. In time, however, states recognized the savings they enjoyed when students enrolled at less costly two-year colleges and began to compensate the school districts that sponsored a junior college for all or part of these savings through a program of state enrollment grants. But it would not be until the 1960s, when the first federal student aid programs made it possible for states to indirectly shift some of their students' tuition costs onto the federal government, that states gained the means to preserve the rhetoric of mass higher education while at the same time generating the required revenue to fund enrollment grants through increased tuition charges without the politically unacceptable necessity of denying access to public higher education to all but the most affluent.

Conclusion

Any honest historian will readily acknowledge the difficulty of drawing any specific lesson from the circumstances that surrounded the funding of early junior colleges that would be of particular relevance to community colleges of the twenty-first century. Junior colleges of some eighty years ago were universally small, exclusive, and expensive—not institutions of ten or twelve thousand students with annual budgets in excess of $10 million and a range of student aid programs to offset tuition costs for those students with documented need. But if one steps back and views the community college in its larger political context, an important, even vital, lesson can be learned. Now, as then, funding of higher education in America remains primarily a state concern, and thus the product of the annual or biannual confrontation of interests that is the state legislative process. Any belief that soundly conceived policy guides legislative decision making, particularly when it comes to the core issue of funding, is simply the post hoc rationalization of this political process. Just as the University of Wyoming sought to block legislative endorsement of junior colleges in the 1930s out of no more lofty a motive than the desire to maintain its enrollment to fill its dormitories, today's advocates of the so-called high tuition and high aid funding policy do nothing more than provide a convenient rationalization for those who would substitute loans for grants—in the full knowledge that disadvantaged students are far more unwilling than the children of affluence to risk a future burdened by loans with no guarantee of employment (McPherson, Schapiro, and Winston, 1993).

If community colleges are to survive the hostile fiscal environment of this century, particularly in the face of seemingly uncontrollable Medicaid mandates, their leaders must learn the lesson of the last—that community colleges are not so much "uniquely American" as "typically American." Their funding, as is the case with all public entities, is the product of the clash of interests that is at the heart of the democratic process, and their leaders will secure whatever funding they seek only to the degree that they act in their institutions' immediate, objective interest and eschew policies grounded in ideology rather than political reality.

This end will not be easily realized. Few institutions in this nation have escaped the ideological polarization that has divided Washington and many state capitals over the last two decades. When Breneman and Nelson (1981) speak of the private benefits of higher education and the legitimacy of charging students full price for those benefits, they are simply reflecting the "ownership" ideology first championed by Reagan and Thatcher in the 1980s.

Although some community college leaders may be committed to the policy of inclusion implicit in such concepts as learning communities and diversity, they place themselves and their institutions in direct conflict with the ownership ideology that continues to dominate much of American political thinking at both the state and federal levels. Looking to the future, one cannot help but expect growing conflict between these two ideologies, for as it is clear to any Marxist, both are riddled with contradictions and neither can claim any grounding in two-year college history. The only hope to free community colleges and their students from this conflict is to focus on its past as past—the province of historians—and not as prologue—the instrument of ideologues. By giving greater attention to the message of primary sources, and discounting the self-interested pronouncements of such figures as Zook and Koos, we may better understand the objective conditions that gave rise to the two-year college, rekindle that remarkable creativity in funding that kept junior colleges alive despite entrenched opposition, and put aside the mining of their past solely for confirmation of current ideological interests.

References

Breneman, D. W., and Nelson, S. C. *Financing Community Colleges: An Economic Perspective.* Washington, D.C.: Brookings Institution, 1981.

Brick, M. "The American Association of Junior Colleges: Forum and Focus for the Junior College Movement." Unpublished doctoral dissertation, Teachers College, Columbia University, 1963.

Brint, S., and Karabel, J. *The Diverted Dream.* New York: Oxford University Press, 1989.

Charters, W. W. "Functions of the Junior College." *Bulletin of the Department of Secondary School Principals of the National Education Association,* 1929, *13*(25), 300–307.

Cotton, M. "The Local Public Junior College in Oklahoma." Unpublished master's thesis, University of Oklahoma, 1929.

Foote, J. "The Junior College Movement in Louisiana." Louisiana State Department of Education bulletin no. 11, 1928.

Greenleaf, W. *The Cost of Going to College.* Pamphlet no. 52. Washington, D.C.: Bureau of Education, 1934.

Hansen, W., and Weisbrod, B. *Benefits, Costs, and Finance of Public Higher Education.* New York: Markham, 1969.

Hardin, T. L. "A History of the Community Junior College in Illinois: 1901–1972." Unpublished doctoral dissertation, University of Illinois, Urbana, 1975.

Hedgepeth, V. "The Six-Year High School Plan at Goshen, Indiana." *School Review,* Jan. 1905, *13*, 19–23.

Hurt, H. W. *The College Blue Book.* Hollywood-by-the-Sea, Fla.: College Blue Book Company, 1928.

Joyal, A. "Factors Relating to the Establishment and Maintenance of Junior Colleges, with Special Reference to California." *University of California Publications in Education,* 1932, *6*, 361–418.

"The Junior College Movement." *American Educational Digest,* Dec. 1927, *47*, 171–173.

Koos, L. *The Junior College.* Minneapolis: University of Minnesota, 1924.

Lahti, R. E. "A Review of Junior-College Development in Wyoming and a Statistical Comparison of Academic Performance of Junior-College Transfer Students and Native Students at the University of Wyoming." Unpublished doctoral dissertation, University of Wyoming, 1961.

Lange, A. F. "The Junior College, with Special Reference to California." *Education Administration and Supervision,* Jan. 1916, 2, 1–8.

Levine, D. *The American College and the Culture of Aspiration: 1915–1940.* Ithaca, N.Y.: Cornell University Press, 1986.

McPherson, M., Schapiro, M., and Winston, G. *Paying the Piper: Productivity, Incentives, and Financing in U.S. Higher Education.* Ann Arbor: University of Michigan Press, 1993.

Prall, C. E. "Report of the Junior College Survey Committee." *Journal of Arkansas Education,* 1930, 9(2), 18–23.

Proctor, W. M. "California's Contributions to the Junior College Movement." In W. M. Proctor (ed.), *The Junior College: Its Organization and Administration.* Palo Alto, Calif.: Stanford University Press, 1927.

Senate Journal of the Twenty-First Legislature. Seattle: State of Washington, 1929.

Turner, E. C. "Schools—Authority of Legislature to Establish Schools and Colleges—Authority of Boards of Education—Junior Colleges." *Ohio Opinions of the Attorney General,* 1928, 3(2017), 1013–1016.

Veysey, L. *The Emergence of the American University.* Chicago: University of Chicago Press, 1965.

Winchell, K. "Junior Colleges in Wyoming." *Junior College Journal,* 1931, 1(9), 540.

Wyoming Community College Records Manual. Cheyenne: Wyoming State Archives, Museum and Historical Department, n.d.

Zook, G. F. "The Junior College." *School Review,* Oct. 1922, 30, 574–83.

Zook, G. F. "Report of Committee on Junior Colleges." *Transactions of the Ohio College Association's 57th Annual Meeting,* 1928, 44, 3–4.

ROBERT PEDERSON *is an independent scholar based in Maryland. He maintains the Web site www.junior-college-history.org to assist scholars and doctoral students interested in the early documentary history of the two-year college.*

2

This chapter describes the dramatically changed external landscape in which community college leaders pursue state dollars and details how other spending priorities in health care, K–12 education, and corrections negatively affect the states' ability to fund community colleges.

Increased Competition for Scarce State Dollars

Stephen G. Katsinas

As a result of the recent recession and decline in state revenues, many state legislatures consider funding public institutions of higher education only after they have funded other major programs in the state budget. As a discretionary item, public colleges are generally funded with monies left on the table after more pressing state priorities, such as matching programs—especially Medicaid—that attract large amounts of federal funds, have been dealt with and such functions as corrections and K–12 education have been provided for. This has not always been the case. During the 1960s and 1970s when the baby-boom generation went to college, higher education enjoyed a "favored position" in states, and community college leaders looked optimistically to state legislatures for badly needed support (Tillery and Wattenbarger, 1985). States' capacity or willingness to provide that support has since diminished, and community colleges have had to adapt in ways that can run counter to their ideals of increasing access and equity.

In this chapter, I explore how increased competition from K–12 education, health care, and corrections, as well as the tax limitation movement and the rise of a "private benefits" model of higher education, have produced structural state budget deficits and new ground rules for obtaining state support for community college operating budgets. I begin by tracing the historical roots of these changes, to show how they have led to a change in the ways states deal with the recessions and structural deficits that together have made higher education vulnerable to further cuts in state support.

NEW DIRECTIONS FOR COMMUNITY COLLEGES, no. 132, Winter 2005 © Wiley Periodicals, Inc.   19

Advocacy for Public Higher Education Weakens in a Post–Vietnam War Power Vacuum

Community colleges have seen dramatic changes in the ground rules under which they have been financed since the baby boomers attended college between 1960 and 1975. During those years, private fundraising, now aggressively pursued by community colleges and other institutions of higher education, was a peripheral activity (Keener, Carrier, and Meaders, 2002). As one long-retired community college president recently told me, "We flatly refused to engage in private fundraising, because we believed we were *state-supported* institutions [emphasis his] and proud of it. We left individual fundraising to private colleges" (B. J. Priest, personal communication, Aug. 2004). In an era when community college students in states such as Minnesota pay well over $4,000 in tuition and fees, and Pell grants cover an increasingly lower portion of the total costs of attending college (McKeon, 2002), the optimistic expectation articulated by Breneman and Nelson (1981) that ever-increasing federal support for financial aid would sustain low tuitions now seems quaint. Times have changed.

Commentators have often referred to the 1960s as a golden age for state support of public higher education (Kerr, 1991; Lombardi, 1973). However, late-1960s and early-1970s protests against the Vietnam War at public flagship universities provoked a number of direct and indirect negative reactions among state legislatures and governors. Governors Ronald Reagan in California and Richard Ogilvie in Illinois, for example, ran for office on platforms to "clean up the mess" on public college campuses (Dalleck, 2000; Pensoneau, 1997). A more interventionist attitude toward higher education followed that, although initially aimed at flagship universities, set the stage for today's more distrustful relationship between state governments and community colleges.

The formalization of state coordinating boards for public higher education, mandated by Section 1202 of the Education Amendments in the 1972 reauthorization of the federal Higher Education Act of 1965, occurred at roughly the same time as the Vietnam War unrest. During the 1950s and 1960s, public flagship university presidents were informally assigned the task of pulling together all education sectors—K–12, junior colleges, and regional universities—to present a unified budget to state legislators and governors. Prior to the 1970s, most legislatures met every other year. The university leaders possessed expert budgeting knowledge, and professional legislative budgetary staffs were small, if they existed at all. State legislators and governors deferred to flagship university leaders to coordinate funding for education (C. L. Choate, personal communication, May 1999). As the Vietnam unrest weakened both the convening and moral authority of university presidents, and shortened flagship university presidential tenure, state coordinating boards came to fill a power vacuum.

Coordinating boards have not advocated as strongly on behalf of public institutions of higher education as flagship presidents once did. Regardless of the type of coordination—consolidated governing boards, combined coordinating boards for community colleges, regional universities, and flagship universities, or dual structures with independent boards for community colleges and universities—these boards are not always successful in providing leadership and advocacy during the "request phase" of the budget process. Indeed, these agencies often have become tools of governors, deliberately choosing not to aggressively pursue the money necessary to meet higher education's fiscal needs, lest new taxes need be raised. During the fourteen years James Thompson served as governor of Illinois (1977 to 1991), the board of higher education he appointed not once proposed a budget that exceeded his initial recommendation. While helping to represent a university in Springfield during Thompson's tenure, I heard critics of his budget proposals say—off the record—that institutional advocacy was trumped by a need to be antitax as a matter of principle. Governors do not often support large spending requests for higher education that require unpopular tax increases. It is politically easier simply to appoint state board members who go along with their budget recommendations, as Thompson's election to four terms attests.

State Spending on Health Care, Corrections, K–12 Education, and Community Colleges

Dramatic increases in spending for health care, corrections, and K–12 education, along with long-term declines in sales tax revenues, have created structural deficits in many state budgets. Until the early 1990s, higher education was the second largest item, after K–12 education, in state budgets. In the late 1960s and early 1970s, funding for K–12 and higher education totaled over 50 percent of total state spending. In fiscal year 1969, K–12 and higher education spending constituted 38 and 17 percent, respectively, of Ohio's total state budget. By fiscal year 1996, those percentages fell to 23 and 10 percent, respectively (Johnson and Katsinas, 1998). In 2002, funding for higher education was approximately 11 percent of total state spending, behind both K–12 and Medicaid (National Governors Association and National Association of State Budget Officers, 2003).

Increased state spending on health care is a primary reason why public institutions of higher education have received a smaller proportion of state budgets in recent years. It is no accident that between 1996 and 1999, when Medicaid costs increased at or below the inflation rate, states were simultaneously able to cut taxes, increase K–12 investments, and increase spending for public higher education. In all other years since 1980, state health care spending has risen by over 6 percent each year, more than double the rate of inflation (Heffler, 2005). This is a major contributing factor to what some higher education budget experts term a "structural state budget deficit" that threatens support for public higher education (Hovey, 1999; Wellman, 2002).

In combination with the steep decline in state revenues that occurred as a result of the 2001 recession, increased state spending on health care has greatly affected the percentage of state budgets available to institutions of higher education. The situation has worsened in recent years: total state expenditures for Medicaid grew 11.6 percent and 11.7 percent in 2001 and 2002, respectively (National Association of State Budget Officers, 2002). This rate is approximately *five times* the projected increase in the consumer price index of 2.0 percent (Bush, 2003). Medicaid *by itself* accounted for 20.1 percent of total state spending in 2000, and 20.7 percent in 2001 (National Governors Association and National Association of State Budget Officers, 2003).

And because the federal government did not control Medicaid costs, the states could not either, because the program is offered to states on a take-it-or-leave-it matching basis. This is why governors of both parties oppose the Bush administration's $60 billion proposed Medicaid cuts over the next decade, as well as efforts to push administrative costs of the new prescription drug law onto states. In his February 2005 speech to the National Governors Association (NGA), President George W. Bush tried to calm governors worried about soaring Medicaid costs. But even Republicans such as Governor Mike Huckabee of Arkansas, the NGA vice chairman, believe that "simply cutting the Medicaid budget is unacceptable" (Pear, 2005, p. 14). Clearly, health care spending is squeezing out state support for community colleges' operating budgets: forty-six of forty-nine reporting state directors of community colleges surveyed in October 2004 indicated that Medicaid costs have become the top budget driver in their state (Katsinas, Palmer, and Tollefson, 2004). There are no large pots of federal matching funds to support community college operating budgets, and thus community colleges become a lower priority.

As a percentage of total state spending, money spent on corrections has also surged in the past two decades. As of December 31, 2001, over two million Americans were incarcerated at federal, state, and local prisons, jails, and other facilities. In 1980, there were only about three hundred thousand; this number grew to roughly seven hundred thousand in 1990 and ballooned during the next decade. Fortunately, the explosive growth rate of incarcerated persons has slowed. According to the Bureau of Justice Statistics (2002), in the last six months of 2001 the number of inmates under state jurisdiction declined by 3,705 (down 0.3 percent), and the 2001 growth rate was the slowest for the nation's prison population since 1972. Therefore, the $29 billion in state corrections spending, which accounted for 3.7 percent of total state spending in 1997, may finally be leveling off.

In the late 1990s, elementary and secondary education expenditures also rose, as a result of three key factors. First, there was an 18 percent increase in pre-K to eighth-grade enrollments in the 1990s, and a 14 percent increase in ninth- to twelfth-grade secondary enrollments. Nearly 6.6 million *more* students were enrolled at the decade's end than at its beginning. Second, new state initiatives such as lower class sizes for primary grades, full-day kindergarten, prekindergarten programs, special education programs, math and science education programs, and alternative high school programs have been added to state budgets. Although worthwhile, these programs carry added costs and produce a larger public education workforce; from 1988 to 1998, public education employment grew by 23.7 percent (Ehrenhalt, 2000). Third, if states are to fully embrace reforms tied to the federal No Child Left Behind Act (NCLB), additional state expenditures on K–12 education will be needed. A study of ten states' experiences implementing NCLB found: "Providing a 'standards-based' NCLB education for all children will require massive new investments in education spending. Public spending on K–12 education was $422.7 billion in 2001–02. If we use a broad—yet easily justified and extremely conservative—estimate of 20 percent added costs for the nation as a whole, that translates into a national increase of about $84.5 billion. An estimate of 35 percent additional costs yields a national increase of $148 billion" (Mathis, 2003, pp. 680–681). Increased K–12 spending required by NCLB, along with health care and corrections spending, places community colleges well down the state budget food chain.

The Antitax Movement and the Rise of a Private Benefits Model

An antitax movement, a term limits movement, and the rise of a private benefits model of higher education have also influenced the states' capacity to fund community colleges. In 1979, California voters approved Proposition 13, a constitutional amendment limiting property taxes. This marked the start of a national antitax movement, of which the term limits movement was a part, to decrease the size of government. This shift toward smaller government was of seismic proportions. Gone was the traditional Republican idea to push government programs and services from federal to state and local governments, as Earl Warren or Nelson Rockefeller promoted in California and New York (Cray, 1997; Warren, 1977). No longer was Abraham Lincoln's Republican notion of government as an instrument to do more conveniently for the people what they could not do for themselves accepted. Instead, a radical *new federalism* emerged, which argued that government itself is inherently bad, and the less of it, the better.

Such rhetoric did not auger well for federal or state investments in higher education. In 1982, higher education lobbyists prevented the Reagan administration from ending federal funding of student aid. But the era of continuous increases in Pell grants was over. With the President's blessing, Grover Norquist, a former Reagan political adviser, founded Americans for

Tax Reform (ATR) in 1986. According to its Web site (Americans for Tax Reform, n.d.-a), "ATR opposes all tax increases as a matter of principle. We believe in a system in which taxes are simpler, fairer, flatter, more visible, and lower than they are today. The government's power to control one's life derives from its power to tax. We believe that power should be minimized" (n.p.). Since 1986, ATR has sponsored its "State Taxpayer Protection Pledge," which commits signers for federal and state office to oppose tax increases: "I [name] pledge to the taxpayers of the [district #] district, of the state of [state], and to all the people of this state, that I will oppose and vote against any and all efforts to increase taxes" (Americans for Tax Reform, n.d.-b, n.p.). As of November 1, 2004, 1,332 state legislators and eight governors had signed the pledge, and in twenty-five states at least 20 percent of one legislative house had signed it (Americans for Tax Reform, 2004). These twenty-five include both "red" and "blue" states, an indication of the national character of the antitax movement.

The ATR pledge allows signers to increase user fees (including tuition) according to the following narrow definition: "To qualify as a fee, a charge must fund a specific service, with no excess going into a general fund; the charge must be paid only by those who use that specific government service; and individuals must have the choice whether to purchase that service from the government (and thus pay the fee) or to purchase the service from a private business. Excise taxes, sales taxes, or taxes levied on businesses to pay for government regulation are *not* user fees" (Americans for Tax Reform, n.d.-b, n.p.). ATR opposes increasing taxes to ameliorate sharp declines in state revenues, such as those that occurred in the 2001 recession, justifying its position as follows: "Tax-and-spend politicians often use 'emergencies' to justify increasing taxes. In the unfortunate event of a *real* crisis or natural disaster, legislators should cut spending in other areas instead of aggravating the situation" (Americans for Tax Reform, n.d.-c, n.p.).

The rise of the antitax movement coincides with the beginning of flat funding for federal student aid programs and a long-term decline in state investment in public higher education, both aspects of a private benefits model of higher education funding. The Pell grant, which funded two-thirds or more of total community college costs in the early 1980s, funds less than 40 percent today (Mortensen, 2003). Sharply rising public university tuitions motivated Representative H. P. "Buck" McKeon (R-Calif.) to propose federal legislation to reduce federal need-based student aid funding to states if tuition increased over the rate of inflation for a set period of time (McKeon, 2003).

Directly linking federal student aid for financially needy students to in-state tuition levels ignores the more complex, comprehensive web of relationships between states and the various cabinet-level agencies of the national government in our federalist system. Other demands on state budgets far exceed the demand to fund public higher education. If states are unwilling to raise taxes, the lower funds they send to institutions give college boards and administrations no choice but to raise tuition in order to sustain their operating budgets. Although higher education is the third largest item in state government budgets, its discretionary nature makes its funding quite vulnerable to economic downswings. The rise of the antitax movement has meant that state governments are far less likely to temporarily raise taxes to ameliorate short-term revenue shortages that occur during recession, a point evidenced by the fact that in thirty-four states, community colleges experienced midyear budget cuts in spring 2003 (Katsinas and Palmer, 2003).

Traditional Methods to Deal with Recession No Longer Apply

The diminished voice of higher education in state budget battles and the rise of a private benefits model of funding coincided with the beginning of a long period of fiscal turbulence, which severely challenged the "wait-it-out" approach typically taken by states during economic downturns. Since the Vietnam War, Americans have endured four recessions: 1973–74, 1979 to 1982, 1990–91, and 2001. Prior to 1980, state budget shortfalls were met by combinations of spending cuts and temporary revenue increases. This made sense because of external economic structures and internal state expenditure flows. Much of the post–World War II economy was manufacturing-based, and the New Deal–era unemployment insurance system, which assumed the same jobs would return at recession's end, provided funds to tide workers over between dips in employment. The shift from manufacturing to an information-based economy, however, meant many jobs would never return (Nardone, Herz, Mellor, and Hipple, 1993).

Changes in the structures of state budgets also took their toll, especially in recessions. Prior to 1980, when K–12 and higher education together commanded over 50 percent of total spending, state leaders responded to recessions by "flat-funding" every item in the state budget, including education, limiting employee pay increases, and cutting spending where possible (for example, by delaying capital expenditures). Institutions could raise tuition and other user fees to close the remaining budget gap. If the gap was larger, temporary tax increases (most often, sales taxes) could be imposed. When K–12 and higher education constituted 55 to 60 percent of total state budgets, this was relatively easy to do. Today, however, because K–12 and higher education together make up less than a third of total state expenditures, it is simply not possible to meet a major shortfall in state revenues by raiding higher education (Katsinas and Palmer, 2003).

The antitax movement also put pressure on state budgets during recessions. Like Proposition 13 in California, many states have enacted laws to make even temporary tax increases more difficult to institute quickly. As a result, recessions are more severe because states do not protect their public higher education operating budgets, including community colleges, from the ebbs and flows of the economy by temporarily raising taxes.

How have changes in the structure of state budgets and an increasingly antitax environment affected community colleges? Prior to the 1980s and the advent of the information age, a general rule of thumb was that enrollment at community colleges was inversely related to employment levels. When times were good, people chose good jobs at good wages over seeking further education and training at community colleges. When times were bad, laid-off workers enrolled at community colleges to retool their skill sets. This pattern, in large measure, reflected the manufacturing-based economy in which workers with high school diplomas could obtain well-paying unionized jobs and enter the nation's middle class.

A rapidly changing information economy, however, produced a continuous churning of jobs, longer periods of sustained unemployment, and job loss. Bureau of Labor Statistics economists Nardone, Herz, Mellor, and Hipple (1993) found that in recessions prior to 1990–91, employees not expecting to be recalled to their jobs never accounted for more than three-fifths of laid-off workers. "Since 1990, however, this group has represented about nine-tenths of the increase in unemployment stemming from job loss. And in 1992 alone, permanent job losers have made up most of the net increase in unemployment" (p. 10). Thus, beginning in the mid-1980s, demands for community college education were no longer tied directly to economic cycles of expansion and contraction. Rather, demand has consistently expanded, fueled not only by "Tidal Wave II"—the dramatic increase in graduates from the nation's high schools—but also by workers continuously returning to community colleges for shorter-term, nondegree or noncredit training.

Although no set of institutions in American society is formally charged to serve currently employed workers who want to augment their skills simply to maintain their present jobs, community colleges have largely accepted this role as one of their multiple missions. Noncredit enrollments exceed 40 percent of the total, or 5 million of the 11.6 million community college students nationally (American Association of Community Colleges, 2000). This role was ushered in by the federal Job Training Partnership Act of 1982, which created an accessible stream of federal funds (Katsinas and Swender, 1994), although such funding has been flat in recent years. Because federal data tracking systems cannot document this noncredit training function (Katsinas, 1994), it is much more difficult for college leaders to make their case for funding before Congress and state legislatures. At a time when the states' capacity to fund higher education has become more tenuous and demands for workforce training are increasing, workforce training is an unfunded mandate. As Donna Hackett of the North Orange County Community College District said, "Our enrollment fluctuates with employment rates. This is one of the few times when our enrollment is down not because of a lack of demand but because of a restriction in our resources" (Shek, 2003, n.p.).

Addressing Today's State Budget Deficits:
Implications for Community College Leaders

Hovey (1999) argues that unless states raise taxes to address structural budget deficits, funding will become even more volatile because allocations earmarked for public higher education will be raided to serve other state needs in bad economic times. Hovey's argument has proven true in the current recession. Expenditures on K–12 education, health care, and corrections would have to be held nearly constant in order to accommodate the increase in projected college enrollments associated with "Tidal Wave II." Yet this has not occurred. Instead, many governors and state legislatures "spread the pain" by cutting appropriations to all public higher education sectors on an across-the-board basis. Because community colleges are more dependent on state funds than other sectors of higher education (Hebel, 2003), reductions hurt more than they do at four-year colleges and universities. At the institutional level, state funding reductions challenge governing boards to make up the difference by raising local revenues, cutting programs, or both. Raising local revenues through tuition and fees and local taxes shifts the costs from the state to local taxpayers, students, and their families. Cutting costs usually means reducing faculty and staff, for personnel costs are four-fifths of institutional operating budgets. In 2003, all forty-five state directors of community colleges surveyed by Katsinas and Palmer (2003) reported tuition increases, and forty-four of forty-seven reported increases in 2004 (Katsinas, Palmer, and Tollefson, 2004). In both years, tuition rose at a rate greater than the 2.0 percent inflation projected for the consumer price index.

Due to growing enrollments and state budget cuts, community colleges are being forced to make tough choices and do more with less. In addition, the rise of term limits in twenty-two states has negatively affected the legislature's collective memory of the rationale for formula funding of community colleges. Often, compromises built into state formulas are totally forgotten or ignored. Texas, for example, never fully funded the instructional portion of its formula. Amazingly, even though Texas counts tuition paid by students and families as part of the state's share, support for community colleges dropped from 81 percent in 1994–95 to 52 percent in 2004–05. A total of $357 million is needed just to restore the cuts made at the recession's height in 2002–03, when Texas funded 65 percent of the formula (Texas Association of Community Colleges, 2005). Steep cuts in funding directly conflict with Texas's stated policy goal to close gaps in the participation rates of its fast-growing Hispanic population by enrolling 370,000 additional community college students between 2000 and 2015 (Texas Higher Education Coordinating Board, 2000).

Unfortunately, the plight of other states is similar. Even states with historically low levels of investment in community colleges have seen sharp declines in state funding. Indeed, Katsinas and Palmer (2003) found that states with high levels of local taxation sustained even deeper cuts than states without local taxation. This may occur because state budgeters know community college districts have access to local revenues, and shift costs from state to local sources in order to make deeper cuts in the statewide budget. In these difficult and often cynical funding environments, community college leaders and boards of trustees must either dramatically increase tuition rates, cut programs, or both. But what happens when a community college district lacks one of the two key prerequisites of financial sustainability—access to a viable local revenue stream, and citizens willing to tax themselves? Colleges without access to local revenue streams may be forced to cut high-cost, high-tech programs such as allied health, nursing, or statistical numerical control machining—despite research showing these programs critical to their regional economies. Raising tuition, then, is the only option left, yet that can depress student enrollment, especially for the disadvantaged, thus depriving students of the opportunity to gain the lifelong skills critical to employment in an information economy.

The effects of rapid increases in tuition can be seen in Minnesota. In 1989, Minnesota ranked first among all states in the percentage of its eighteen- to twenty-four-year-olds enrolled in college. By 2003 its ranking had slipped to seventeenth, as tuition at its community and technical colleges exceeded the maximum Pell grant of $4,000 (Martinez, 2004; Minnesota State Colleges and Universities, 2005). Because the dollar amount of the federal Pell grant has not been increased since 2000, a similar trend may occur in other states. Unless state higher education policy actually favors fewer young people going on to college, it seems that the conflict between practice and policy may increase in future years. Sadly, poor students today must take out increasingly large student loans to graduate, requiring community colleges and access-oriented four-year institutions to teach them financial debt management (Short, 2005).

In 2003 and again in 2004, my colleagues and I asked state directors of community colleges which functions would be strengthened, level-funded, or cut in the following year of the budget cycle. In 2003, the number of states predicting declines was larger than the number of states predicting increases for each of the following five community college functions: general education and transfer; vocational, occupational, and technical education; continuing education; community services and workforce training; and developmental education (Katsinas and Palmer, 2003). The budgetary situation was improved in 2004, when thirteen of the forty-eight responding state directors indicated that general education would be strengthened; thirty-three predicted flat-funding, and only two indicated that there would be cuts. Similar responses were reported for other functions except for developmental education and federally funded workforce training; in these two areas, states predicting that funding would be weakened outnumbered those predicting that funding would decline (Katsinas, Palmer, and Tollefson, 2004).

At the institutional level, the external funding environment does not bode well for the future of developmental education. A September 2002 study of developmental education by the Center for Community College Policy of the Education Commission of the States found thirty-seven states reporting that 79 percent of students entering community colleges would need some form of developmental education (Jenkins and Boswell, 2002). If states cut funding for developmental education, colleges may be forced either to reduce this function and thereby close the open door or to make other tough choices regarding reduction of functions to substitute for declining state investment. Institutions at greatest risk of reducing developmental education are likely those in states with local taxes, and at rural community colleges, which—in both 2003 and 2004—state directors reported as facing the greatest financial strain by wide margins (Katsinas and Palmer, 2003; Katsinas, Palmer, and Tollefson, 2004).

Conclusion

Over the past decade, community colleges have been mentioned by name in most presidential State of the Union addresses. President George W. Bush's 2005 reference to community colleges produced a sustained standing ovation. Sadly, presidential attention does not translate into hard dollars to finance preservation—much less expansion—of the open door college. For those who see community colleges as critical portals to the baccalaureate, and who are concerned with access to an education that can prepare and retrain workers for jobs in the knowledge economy, the current situation is troubling. Structural state budget deficits caused by skyrocketing increases in health care, corrections, and K–12 expenditures threaten community college operating budgets, as do the antitax and private benefits movements, and institutions' diminished capacity to lobby effectively for increased funding. The financing mechanisms used to fund community college operating budgets increasingly conflict with the goal of universal access to postsecondary education. Addressing these issues will challenge community college leaders in future years.

References

American Association of Community Colleges. National Profile of Community Colleges: Trends and Statistics, 2000 (3rd ed.). Washington, D.C.: Community College Press, 2000.

Americans for Tax Reform. "ATR Opposes All Tax Increases as a Matter of Principle." Washington, D.C.: Americans for Tax Reform, n.d.-a. http://www.atr.org/home/about/index.html. Accessed Aug. 12, 2005.

Americans for Tax Reform. "State Taxpayer Protection Pledge." Washington, D.C.: Americans for Tax Reform, n.d.-b. http://www.atr.org/pledge/state/index.html. Accessed Aug. 12, 2005.

Americans for Tax Reform. "Q & A on the Pledge." Washington, D.C.: Americans for Tax Reform, n.d.-c. http://www.atr.org/pledge/national/questions.html. Accessed Aug. 12, 2005.

Americans for Tax Reform. "2003–2004 State Incumbents: State Pledge Signers (as of November 1, 2004)." Washington, D.C.: Americans for Tax Reform, 2004. http://www.atr.org/content/pdf/2004/oct/IncumbentStateSigners2004new.pdf. Accessed Aug. 12, 2005.

Breneman, D. W., and Nelson, S. C. Financing Community Colleges: An Economic Perspective. Washington, D.C.: Brookings Institution, 1981.

Bureau of Justice Statistics. "State Prison Population Drops in Second Half of 2001, Federal Inmate Growth Continues." Press release. Washington, D.C.: U.S. Department of Justice, July 30, 2002. http://www.ojp.usdoj.gov/bjs/pub/press/p01pr.htm. Accessed Aug. 12, 2005.

Bush, G. W. Economic Report of the President, Transmitted to the Congress, February 2003. Washington, D.C.: U.S. Government Printing Office, 2003. http://www.gpoaccess.gov/usbudget/fy04/pdf/2003_erp.pdf#search='Economic%20Report%20of%20the%20President,%202003'. Accessed Aug. 26, 2005.

Cray, E. Chief Justice: A Biography of Earl Warren. New York: Simon & Schuster, 1997.

Dalleck, M. The Right Moment: Ronald Reagan's First Victory and the Decisive Turning Point in American Politics. New York: Free Press, 2000.

Ehrenhalt, S. M. Public Education: A Major American Growth Industry in the 1990s. Albany, N.Y.: Nelson A. Rockefeller Institute of Government, 2000. http://www.rockinst.org/publications/fiscal_studies/PubEducEhrenhalt.PDF. Accessed June 26, 2003.

Hebel, S. "Unequal Impact—Community Colleges Face Disproportionate Cuts in State Budgets." Chronicle of Higher Education, May 30, 2003, pp. A1, A21.

Heffler, S. "National Health Expenditures (NHE) Growth, 1980–2014." Washington, D.C.: Health Affairs/Kaiser Family Foundation Forum, 2005. http://www.kaisernetwork.org/health_cast/uploaded_files/022305hefflerpresentation.pdf. Accessed Aug. 16, 2005.

Hovey, H. A. State Spending for Higher Education in the Next Decade: The Battle to Sustain Current Support. National Center report no. 99–3. Washington, D.C.: National Center for Public Policy and Higher Education, 1999. http://www.nchems.org/State_Spending_Hovey.pdf. Accessed Feb. 28, 2005.

Jenkins, D., and Boswell, K. State Policies on Community College Remedial Programs: Findings from a National Survey. Denver: Education Commission of the States, Center for Community College Policy, 2002. http://www.ecs.org/clearinghouse/40/81/4081.pdf. Accessed June 26, 2003.

Johnson, J. L., and Katsinas, S. G. "State Underfunding of Public Higher Education in the Great Lakes States: An Overview with Emphasis on Ohio." Toledo Journal of the Great Lakes, Fall 1998, pp. 211–243.

Katsinas, S. G. "Is the Open Door Closing? The Democratizing Role of the Community College in the Post–Cold War Era." Community College Journal, 1994, 64(5), 22–28.

Katsinas, S. G., and Palmer, J. C. State Funding for Community Colleges: A View from the Field. Denton: University of North Texas, Bill J. Priest Center for Community College Education, 2003. http://www.unt.edu/Priest/Presentations/ACCT%20presentation2003.pdf. Accessed Aug. 16, 2005.

Katsinas, S. G., Palmer, J. C., and Tollefson, T. A. State Funding for Community Colleges: A View from the Field. Denton: University of North Texas, Bill J. Priest Center for Community College Education, 2004.

Katsinas, S. G., and Swender, H. J. "Community Colleges and JTPA: Involvement and Opportunity." Community, Technical, and Junior College Journal, 1994, 62(6), 18–23.

Keener, B. J., Carrier, S. M., and Meaders, S. J. "Resource Development in Community Colleges: A National Overview." Community College Journal of Research and Practice, 2002, 26(1), 7–23.

Kerr, C. *The Great Transformation in Higher Education, 1960–1980.* Albany: State University of New York Press, 1991.

Lombardi, J. "Critical Decade for Community College Financing." In J. Lombardi (ed.), *Meeting the Financial Crisis.* New Directions for Community Colleges, no. 2. San Francisco: Jossey-Bass, 1973.

Martinez, M. C. *Meeting the Challenges of Population Growth and the Future Demand for Postsecondary Education, Considerations for State Higher Education Policy.* Policy brief PS-04–05W. Denver: Education Commission of the States, 2004.

Mathis, W. J. "No Child Left Behind: Costs and Benefits." *Phi Delta Kappan,* 2003, *84*(9), 679–686. http://www.pdkintl.org/kappan/k0305mat.htm#27a. Accessed June 26, 2004.

McKeon, H. P. "Opening Statement of Congressman Howard P. 'Buck' McKeon." *Access to Higher Education for Low-Income Students: A Review of the Advisory Committee on Student Financial Assistance Report on College Access.* Hearing before the Committee on Education and the Workforce, House of Representatives, 107th Cong., 2nd sess., July 16, 2002, Serial no. 107–71. Washington, D.C.: U.S. Government Printing Office, 2002. http://www.ed.gov/about/bdscomm/list/acsfa/ephearing.pdf. Accessed May 18, 2005.

McKeon, H. P. "Colleges Can Do More to Hold Down Prices, Congress Told." Press release. Sept. 23, 2003. http://mckeon.house.gov/News/DocumentSingle.aspx?DocumentID=6362. Accessed May 18, 2005.

Minnesota State Colleges and Universities. "Information for Students. College Cost Comparison. Annual Tuition and Fees 2004–2005." St. Paul: Minnesota State Colleges and Universities, 2005. http://www.mnscu.edu/students/tuition/collegecost comparison.html. Accessed May 18, 2005.

Mortensen, T. A. "Distribution of Pell Grant Recipients by Institutional Type and Control by State 1992–93 to 2001–02." Oskaloosa, Iowa: Postsecondary Education OPPORTUNITY, 2003. http://www.postsecondary.org/archives/Reports/Spreadsheets/pellrecipbytype.htm. Accessed May 18, 2005.

Nardone, T., Herz, D., Mellor, E., and Hipple, S. "1992: Job Market in the Doldrums." *Monthly Labor Review,* 1993, *116*(2), 3–14.

National Association of State Budget Officers. *NASBO Analysis: Medicaid to Stress State Budgets Severely into Fiscal 2003.* Washington, D.C.: National Association of State Budget Officers, 2002. http://www.nasbo.org/Publications/PDFs/medicaid2003.pdf. Accessed Feb. 28, 2005.

National Governors Association and the National Association of State Budget Officers. *Fiscal Survey of the States.* Washington, D.C.: National Governors Association and the National Association of State Budget Officers, 2003. http://www.nasbo.org/Publications/fiscalsurvey/fs-spring2003.pdf. Accessed Aug. 12, 2005.

Pear, R. "Governors Resist Bush's Appeal for Quick Deal on Medicaid." *New York Times,* Mar. 1, 2005, p. A14. http://query.nytimes.com/gst/abstract.html?res=F50B17FA 39590C728CDDAA0894DD404482. Accessed Aug. 29, 2005.

Pensoneau, T. *Governor Richard Ogilvie: In the Interest of the State.* Carbondale: Southern Illinois University Press, 1997.

Shek, K. "California Budget Crisis Drives Down Enrollment." *Community College Times,* Sept. 15, 2003, n.p. http://www.aacc.nche.edu/Template.cfm?Section=Enrollment &template=/ContentManagement/ContentDisplay.cfm&ContentID=11115&InterestC ategoryID=248&Name=Enrollment&ComingFrom=InterestDisplay. Accessed Aug. 29, 2005.

Short, J. M. "Consumer Awareness: The Other Half of the Financial Literacy Equation." Presentation at the Spring 2005 Conference of the Ohio Association of Student Financial Aid Administrators, Akron, May 2005. http://www.oasfaa.org/docs/events_training/conference_Spring2005/Handouts/FinancialLiteracyEquation.ppt. Accessed Aug. 26, 2005.

Texas Association of Community Colleges. "Legislative Priorities 2005." Austin: Texas Association of Community Colleges, 2005. http://www.tacc.org/pdf/lpd05_final.pdf. Accessed Feb. 28, 2005.

Texas Higher Education Coordinating Board. *Closing the Gaps: The Texas Master Plan for Higher Education, 2000–2015.* Austin: Texas Higher Education Coordinating Board, 2000.

Tillery, D., and Wattenbarger, J. L. "State Power in a New Era: A Threat to Autonomy." In D. Campbell (ed.), *Strengthening Financial Management.* New Directions for Community Colleges, no. 50. San Francisco: Jossey-Bass, 1985.

Warren, E. *The Memoirs of Earl Warren.* Garden City, N.Y.: Doubleday, 1977.

Wellman, J. V. "Weathering the Double Whammy: How Governing Boards Can Negotiate a Volatile Economy and Shifting Enrollments." Washington, D.C.: Association of Governing Boards, 2002. http://www.centerforgovernance.net/pages/whammy.pdf. Accessed May 18, 2005.

STEPHEN G. KATSINAS *is director of the Education Policy Center at The University of Alabama.*

3

This chapter argues that a relatively high tuition, high financial aid policy is the most equitable and efficient way to fund community college operating budgets and promote access.

Seeking the Proper Balance Between Tuition, State Support, and Local Revenues: An Economic Perspective

Richard M. Romano

"Show me the money"—that now-recognizable phrase from the movie *Jerry Maguire*—may well be the common cry of community college presidents across the country. As this volume demonstrates, two-year colleges are looking for new sources of revenue in the face of expanding enrollments and declining state support. Yet tuition is the one source of revenue that all colleges seem reluctant to raise. Why? Because, the argument goes, raising tuition would somehow be inequitable for all of those low-income students who attend the community college. In fact, the biggest problem for public institutions of higher education is not that tuition is too high, but that need-based financial aid is too low. Keeping tuition low subsidizes the education of the rich at the expense of the poor. This chapter explains why most economists would view a relatively high tuition, high aid policy as being both more efficient and more equitable, even at the community college level, than a low tuition policy that applies to all students.

Considering the title of this chapter, one might think that there is some optimal balance between the main sources of revenue for the operating budget. This is not the case. No ideal funding formula exists that can be applied to all states, because funding patterns tend to follow the history, governance, and mission assigned to the community college in any particular state. Nevertheless, in an important analysis of community college finance, Breneman and Nelson (1981) highlighted some economic principles that can guide public policy when changes in funding are being considered. This chapter may be viewed as an update of this perspective in a more recent

NEW DIRECTIONS FOR COMMUNITY COLLEGES, no. 132, Winter 2005 © Wiley Periodicals, Inc.

context. It examines the theory behind the public financing of community colleges and some of its practical implications. It is adapted from a larger study prepared for a conference at Cornell University in October 2003 (Romano, 2003). Although space does not permit us to explore all of the issues examined in that presentation, this chapter concludes with the major policy recommendations from the larger study.

The Economic Perspective

When economists look for criteria that can guide the allocation of scarce resources, they turn to the principles of equity and efficiency. Both principles, as well as three other economic arguments related to community college funding, are discussed in the following paragraphs.

Equity. Equity concerns in higher education often revolve around the questions of who benefits from it and who pays for it. Theories that would lead us to the most equitable solution to problems have to do with normative issues concerning fairness and the distribution of income in society and are less precise than those underlying the principles of efficiency. Because income in every society is unevenly divided, using tax monies to support higher education might be justified on the grounds that not everyone has a fair opportunity to go to college (a normative judgment in itself). However, the optimal level of subsidy cannot be calculated in any precise way, and ultimately it becomes a political question related to how much the polity wants to redistribute income in the society, if at all. The value judgment that best fits the underlying philosophy of the community college is that tax-financed subsidies that expand educational opportunities to underserved populations, or those that tend to redistribute income in favor of the poor, are preferable. Yet to get a complete picture of equity we need to know not only which income groups benefit from public subsidies but also which groups pay for them. Given our value judgments, tax structures that are more progressive are preferred to those that are regressive.

Progressive tax structures take a higher percentage of income from families at the top of the income distribution than from those at the bottom. Regressive taxes do the opposite. The federal tax structure is mildly progressive because of the progressive income tax. State and local tax structures, however, are mostly regressive because their revenue comes mainly from property and sales taxes that do not take income into account. Although most economists agree to these general principles, there is some disagreement when it comes to ranking the progressivity of the tax structure for each state (Greene and Balkan, 1987, 1991; Kiefer, 1991). Some of this disagreement has to do with the incidence of different kinds of taxes (or who actually bears the burden of them), but generally we find that state governments that rely more on income taxes, like New York, have more progressive structures than those, such as New Hampshire, that rely more heavily on property taxes. Local tax structures are the most regressive because they generally rely on property and sales taxes rather than income taxes. Although arguments over tax structures are beyond the scope of this chapter, we can conclude that if we want to finance higher education out of tax revenue, and if the desired effect is to collect revenue in the most progressive, or the least regressive, manner, in most cases it will be more equitable to use federal funds first, then state, and finally local sources.

It is widely understood that students who attend the community college are more likely to be from lower income groups than students who go directly to four-year colleges. Yet we know that middle- and upper-income students also attend. In fact, figures from the National Center for Education Statistics (U.S. Department of Education, 2002) show that for 1999–2000, only 16.9 percent of students enrolled in credit courses received Pell grants. However, because of the high number of part-time and nonmatriculated students enrolled at the community college, this low Pell grant rate is not a good proxy for family income levels. Still, even adjusting for these factors, I have calculated that probably less than 30 percent of students have family incomes low enough to qualify for Pell grants (see Romano and Millard, 2005, for more information on this calculation). From the data that we have, it appears that the majority of students who attend the community college are not from the poorer segments of the population. Thus, to the extent that the state and local taxes used to support the community college are paid by lower-income families and are not used by them proportionally in attending, there is a redistribution of income from lower to higher income groups. Because a "free" or very low tuition policy that provides an across-the-board subsidy to all students redistributes income in the wrong direction, it would be better to charge a higher tuition to all and to target financial aid to those least able to afford it. From this perspective, a high tuition, high aid policy is more equitable than a low tuition policy applied to all community college students.

Looking at equity from another perspective, a frequently used standard is that equals should be treated equally. In an ideal world that would mean that, for students of similar ability, the likelihood of attending and doing well in college is the same whether they are from low-income families or from upper-income families. Or, we might argue that similar students taking similar programs should get the same subsidy whether they attend a two-year or four-year public college. Likewise, if we are to treat equals equally, we should treat unequals in an appropriately unequal manner. For instance, because public subsidies go to primary and secondary schools in districts with widely unequal tax bases, the state may give a greater subsidy to the poorer districts. Although interdistrict equity is a huge issue at the elementary and secondary level, it is much less of an issue at the community college level. However, a recent study by Dowd and Grant (2003) shows that the presence of local funding (only fourteen states have no local funding) exacerbates differences in funding between community college districts in a state. This study lends support to the argument presented in this chapter that, from an equity perspective, local funding for community colleges should be phased out wherever possible. To the extent that community colleges continue to be financed from local taxes, the state should give some consideration to equalizing the financial resources available.

Allocative Efficiency. Economic efficiency comprises both technical and allocative efficiency. Perhaps the most common conception of efficiency involves producing a good or service of a given quality at the lowest cost. This is technical efficiency. Applied to the public financing of higher education, technical efficiency might involve the question: Are the costs of educating students lower at a community college than at a four-year college, and do you get the same quality product at the end? On the campus level, technical efficiency would be promoted by providing incentives to use a given level of resources wisely.

However, efficiency is not solely concerned with the lowest cost alternative but also has to do with how society's scarce resources are allocated in accordance with producers' and consumers' choices that balance the costs of producing a good or service against its presumed benefits. Normally, economists prefer to leave decisions about what to produce to individuals interacting through private markets. However, competitive private markets sometimes result in the overproduction of some goods and services and the underproduction of others. This is what economists call a market failure. When we produce the "right" mix of output we have allocative efficiency. However, markets can fail to produce allocative efficiency because some of the costs or benefits are hidden in one way or another from individual decision makers. The case for the public subsidy of education is based on this idea. Without public subsidy, it is argued, higher education would be underproduced, and this would be allocatively inefficient.

Spillovers. In traditional public finance arguments, the idea that an efficient allocation of society's resources is improved by public subsidies to higher education is based on the principle of spillovers and the ideas of imperfect capital markets and imperfect information. The theory of spillovers (sometimes called *neighborhood* or *external effects*) comes from the assumption that the benefits to education are not only private (that is, they flow to the individuals who get it) but also social. It is assumed, equity concerns aside, that because a college education bestows private benefits in the form of higher incomes on individual students, they should bear the cost of that education. Thus, by investing in themselves by going to college, students reap the rewards of their investment through a higher lifetime income. Social benefits, however, are those that spill over to the larger society and cannot be captured by the individual. For example, when people are more educated, they have a greater tolerance for other groups, have lower crime rates, are better able to participate in the democratic process, are more likely to provide volunteer services that contribute to the "social capital" of the community, and are likely to contribute to the productivity of others.

All of these social benefits add up to an increase in the overall public good. However, when individuals consider the costs and benefits of investing in higher education, they do not consider these social benefits, and this causes society to underinvest in education. Because the spillovers from higher education benefit the entire society, we might expect society (through the public sector) to pay for some portion of it. Although little research has examined this question with respect to the community college, the general assumption is that the same sort of benefits ascribed to all of higher education can also be extended to the community college.

If we accept the idea that the justification for some public funding of community colleges is based partly on the idea of spillovers (or neighborhood effects), then we might argue for less of a subsidy for short-term training and avocational courses, because the benefits of these are largely private. In contrast, we might argue for greater subsidies (low or no tuition) for English as a Second Language classes (for local residents but not international students) and remedial education, because these courses have larger spillover effects. Remedial education deserves special attention because of the national trend to shift more of this function to the community college. It appears that the social benefits generated from this type of education are greater than those from, say, general or vocational education. Thus, remediation deserves full public funding (no tuition) with some time limits built in for completion of the program.

In an ideal world we would be able to separate the private from the social benefits for each type of education and set community college tuition accordingly. Or, if we had sufficient knowledge, we could separate the private from the local and the state benefits, and each sector could pay in accordance with the benefits received. In reality we cannot be this precise, and the method of finance becomes a political decision in which the mission of the community college in a particular state, and the priorities assigned to this type of education in the budget process, become the primary considerations. (For an attempt to model this for higher education see Creedy, 1995.)

Stepping back from these theoretical arguments, we can say that for society as a whole, the overriding efficiency question—with respect to the community college—is whether the outcomes (benefits) of this type of education are worth the costs. Again, research on this question is limited, but the preponderance of evidence from studies done in the last ten years indicates that both private and social rates of return are high enough to justify the cost even if students do not complete a degree (Grubb, 1999; Kane and Rouse, 1999; Romano, 1986). Although a detailed examination of this question is beyond the scope of this chapter, we can take the standard view that aside from equity concerns, some degree of public subsidy to community colleges is justified on efficiency grounds, and that if left to private markets exclusively, it would be underproduced.

Imperfect Capital Markets. Imperfect capital markets also contribute to the problem of underinvestment (allocative inefficiency) in the production of educational services. If capital (money) markets were perfect, students who needed financial assistance would be able to obtain the funds for college by taking out a loan, using their future income stream as collateral. Money markets are imperfect, however, because banks are not willing to take such risks, given the long time horizons involved and the uncertain outcome. Therefore, government loan guarantees increase the efficiency with which resources are allocated by providing individuals with a method of making worthwhile investments in themselves through higher education. Similar to the spillover argument, public involvement in private markets through government guarantees of student loans helps make sure that society does not underinvest in higher education.

Imperfect Information. In an important study of the way we finance higher education in the United States, Thomas Kane (1999) suggests a third rationale for public subsidies to higher education on efficiency grounds. According to Kane, some students have poor information about "how to apply to college [and negotiate the financial aid process] and what will be expected of them there" (p. 13). They also lack the information necessary to calculate the net cost (considering financial aid) of attending college. Without public intervention, this imperfect information causes some, particularly low-income students, to underinvest in higher education. According to Kane, improving access to information will not be enough to correct this problem. He suggests that front-loading financial aid—to encourage students on the margin between further schooling and work to experiment with college—would help solve this problem. Kane proposes giving students larger grants during their first two years and smaller grants in the last two years of the typical four-year degree program. In effect, front-loading financial aid, especially for the first year, gives students an incentive to try college and to overcome the often-difficult transition from high school to postsecondary education. Kane is not arguing for an increase in the total amount of federal and state aid, but rather for a reallocation of existing dollars so that "the incremental gain in educational attainment (or, more accurately, in the public good generated by educational attainment) for each dollar of financial aid given college freshmen equals the incremental gain for each dollar of financial aid for college seniors" (1999, p. 13). This recommendation seems to have particular relevance to the students on the margin that the community college generally serves.

Thus far I have argued that the principles of efficiency and equity lead us to the judgment that a high tuition, high aid policy is better than a no or low tuition policy for most courses offered by the community college. However, the proportion of the operating budget that should be covered by tuition cannot be determined in any precise way. When Garms examined this issue in 1977, he recommended that tuition cover 50 percent of operating costs. When Breneman and Nelson (1981) examined the issue, they suggested that 33 percent of the operating budget might be covered by tuition. I found nothing in my study (Romano, 2003) to improve on this estimate, and conclude that the proper ratio is somewhere between 30 and

40 percent, rather than the 1998–99 national average of 21 percent. This higher rate better reflects the private benefits generated by a community college education, and is a more equitable rate of tuition for those who can afford to pay for their education. The relatively wide range of 30 to 40 percent is based on a crude estimate of the differing program mixes found among the nation's comprehensive community colleges.

Technical Efficiency. Although it will not be dealt with here, the larger study from which this chapter is drawn paid some attention to the questions of technical efficiency. For example, is it less expensive to educate a student at a two-year than a four-year college? The answer to that question is yes, but not by as much as you might expect by looking at the average costs per student at each institution. Following an argument advanced by Rouse (1998), my national study concluded that it costs about $1,000 to $1,500 less to educate a student for the first two years at a community college than it does to educate the same student at a public four-year university. If we expect prices to reflect costs (another economic principle), tuition at community colleges should be about $1,000 to $1,500 lower than at their four-year counterparts. National data show that this is roughly the case, although each state might be different (Romano, 2003).

Case Studies

In an attempt to look at the criteria of equity and efficiency on the campus level, my larger study examined the percentage of operating budgets covered by federal, state, and local revenues, as well as tuition and fees (before financial aid) for all fifty states in 1998–99. I examined four states in detail: California, selected because it had the lowest reliance (0.8 percent) on tuition; Arizona, because it had the highest reliance (57 percent) on local funding; North Carolina, because it had the highest reliance (75 percent) on state funding; and New York, because it had a fairly even balance between tuition, state support, and local revenue—tuition made up about 34 percent of community college operating budgets in New York (Education Commission of the States, 2000). I collected information through structured interviews with college presidents, system chancellors, and finance people on community college campuses in each of these four states.

Interviews revealed a host of inefficiencies typical of public institutions. Clearly, some states are worse than others, but mandates from the top, inflexible governance structures, and the lack of control over one's budget were frequently cited inefficiencies. Although accountability for public funds is always necessary, costs of operation can be held down if colleges are allowed more budget flexibility. The ability to shift funds between budget lines, for instance, allows campus leaders to direct resources to areas where they are needed most, and the ability to accumulate a limited fund balance allows the colleges to save for a rainy day and reduces the tendency to spend all that they have or lose it. Of the four states in this study, New

York scored the highest in this kind of flexibility. I also found that operating efficiency improved when community college campuses were allowed to keep revenues they generated from tuition and fees, although colleges should not be tempted to let individual departments keep their tuition revenue as some universities now do (Kirp, 2003). Again, colleges in New York were judged to be the best in this regard, with North Carolina and California the worst.

Finally, an interesting, and now obvious, finding was that the greater the reliance on state funding, the greater the negative impact on a community college's operating budget during difficult economic times (see also Betts and McFarland, 1996). In California and North Carolina (and to some extent in Arizona), when state funding was reduced the number of course sections was cut significantly. Under the same circumstances, colleges in New York were able to expand course offerings because students brought enough tuition revenue with them, and the colleges were allowed to keep it to pay for the variable costs of instruction. Thus, in difficult times New York's relatively high tuition, high aid policy did not compromise the goal of access.

Policy Recommendations

This section summarizes the eight major policy recommendations that grew out of my larger study (Romano, 2003).

Raise Tuition and Need-Based Aid. Revenue from tuition and fees should cover 30 to 40 percent of a community college's operating budget. In most cases colleges will have to raise their tuition to meet this percentage, sometimes substantially. Raising tuition will allow states and local governments to cut back on direct subsidies to colleges, but a portion of the money received should be used by the colleges to provide tuition discounts and expand access for lower-income students (for an extension of this idea, see Romano, 2005). Tuition revenues should be high enough to cover the variable costs of instruction so that even in difficult budget years the class schedule can be expanded in areas of high demand.

Allow Community Colleges More Budget Flexibility. Individual community colleges should be allowed to keep their tuition revenue, should be able to shift funds among budget lines without state approval, and should be allowed to carry over a limited fund balance from one year to the next. All of these measures would improve efficiency at the campus level and save money.

Restructure Federal Financial Aid. Federal financial aid policies should be restructured along the lines suggested by Thomas Kane (1999). Simplifying the application process, front-loading Pell grants, improving information about the availability of loans and grants, and making the repayment of loans more contingent on future income will not only help preserve student choice but will afford a greater number of lower-income students the opportunity to enter the system of higher education.

Move Away from Merit-Based Financial Aid. Recently, many states have been shifting financial aid from need-based grants to merit-based aid and tax incentives. These policies, however, only serve to increase inequalities and do not expand educational opportunities for lower-income students. These trends should be reversed to ensure access for all students, regardless of their ability to pay.

Move Away from Local Support. Efficiency suggests that some degree of local financing for community colleges is justified, but principles of equity argue strongly against local funding because operating budgets should be financed out of a less regressive tax base. In most cases, this would require that local support be phased out or at least reduced substantially. Where local funding remains an important source of revenue, state funding should consider compensating for the inequalities in wealth among regions of the state.

Link State Aid to Enrollment in Specific Community College Programs. State aid should be linked to enrollments with some type of averaging to protect colleges during downturns. Full funding (no tuition) should be provided for remedial and English as a Second Language courses (except for international students), but most noncredit avocational courses should not receive a subsidy. Higher levels of funding should be provided for more expensive technical and medical programs that the state feels are vital to local or regional economic development.

Subsidize Two- and Four-Year College Students at the Same Rate. States should provide the same subsidy to students at two-year colleges as they do to lower-division students at four-year universities. The lower cost of operation at the community colleges should be passed on to students in the form of lower tuition.

Treat Funding for Capital Projects Differently. State funding (bonding) for capital projects should cover 100 percent of costs. Training facilities designed to meet the specific needs of local employers, however, should receive some support from them or from other private sources.

Concluding Remarks

This chapter has provided a brief overview of the theory behind the public financing of community colleges. We have not yet discovered an ideal balance between tuition, state support, and local sources of revenue for operating budgets. However, equity concerns suggest that we should shift away from local funding in most areas and move toward a higher tuition, higher need-based aid policy. The danger is that the states will agree to the higher tuition but not the higher aid recommendation (and indeed this is happening). To counter this, college presidents, on a statewide basis, must use the promise of higher tuition as a bargaining chip. In return for voluntarily giving up state or local aid, they should ask for greater budget flexibility and the ability to use some of the increased tuition revenues to offset tuition discounts for lower-income students (Romano, 2005). In this way, greater efficiency, equity, and access will be achieved.

References

Betts, J. R., and McFarland, L. L. "Safe Port in a Storm: The Impact of Labor Market Conditions on Community College Enrollments." *Journal of Human Resources,* 1996, *30*(4), 741–65.

Breneman, D. W., and Nelson, S. C. *Financing Community Colleges: An Economic Perspective.* Washington, D.C.: Brookings Institution, 1981.

Creedy, J. *The Economics of Higher Education.* London: Edward Elgar, 1995.

Dowd, A. C., and Grant, J. L. "Intrastate Variation in Community College Revenues: The Role of Local Financing." Paper presented at the Complex Community College Conference, Cornell University, Ithaca, N.Y., Oct. 2003. http://www.ilr.cornell.edu/cheri/conf/chericonf2003-oct/chericonf2003-oct_07.pdf. Accessed June 16, 2005.

Education Commission of the States. *State Funding for Community Colleges: A 50-State Survey.* Denver: Education Commission of the States, 2000.

Garms, W. I. *Financing Community Colleges.* New York: Teachers College Press, 1977.

Greene, K. V., and Balkan, E. M. "A Comparative Analysis of Tax Progressivity in the United States." *Public Finance Quarterly,* 1987, *15*(4), 397–416.

Greene, K. V., and Balkan, E. M. "A Re-Examination of Comparative Tax Progressivity in the United States." *Public Finance Quarterly,* 1991, *19*(1), 109–14.

Grubb, W. N. *The Economic Benefits of Sub-Baccalaureate Education: Results from National Studies.* New York: Columbia University, Teachers College, Community College Research Center, 1999.

Kane, T. J. *The Price of Admission: Rethinking How Americans Pay for College.* Washington, D.C.: Brookings Institution, 1999.

Kane, T. J., and Rouse, C. E. "The Community College: Educating Students at the Margin Between College and Work." *Journal of Economic Perspectives,* 1999, *13*(1), 63–84.

Kiefer, D. W. "A Comparative Analysis of Tax Progressivity in the United States: A Further Comment." *Public Finance Quarterly,* 1991, *19*(1), 114–16.

Kirp, D. L. *Shakespeare, Einstein, and the Bottom Line: The Marketing of Higher Education.* Cambridge, Mass.: Harvard University Press, 2003.

Romano, R. M. "What Is the Economic Payoff to a Community College Degree?" *Community/Junior College Quarterly of Research and Practice,* 1986, *10*(3), 153–64.

Romano, R. M. "Financing Community Colleges Across the States: An Economic Perspective." Paper presented at the Complex Community College Conference, Cornell University, Ithaca, N.Y., Oct. 2003. http://www.ilr.cornell.edu/cheri/conf/chericonf2003-oct/chericonf2003-oct_08.pdf. Accessed June 16, 2005.

Romano, R. M. "Privatizing the Community College." *Community College Journal,* 2005, *75*(5), 22–26.

Romano, R. M., and Millard, T. "If Community College Students Are So Poor Why Do Only 16.9% of Them Receive Pell Grants?" Paper presented at the Council for the Study of Community Colleges conference, Boston, Apr. 2005. http://www.ilr.cornell.edu/cheri/wp/cheri_wp72.pdf. Accessed Aug. 9, 2005.

Rouse, C. E. "Do Two-Year Colleges Increase Overall Educational Attainment? Evidence from the States." *Journal of Policy Analysis and Management,* 1998, *17*(4), 595–620.

U.S. Department of Education, National Center for Education Statistics. "1999–2000 National Postsecondary Student Aid Study." Washington, D.C.: U.S. Department of Education, 2002. http://nces.ed.gov/das/library/tables_listings/show_nedrc.asp?rt=p&tableID=319. Accessed June 16, 2005.

RICHARD M. ROMANO is director of the Institute for Community College Research at Broome Community College and State University of New York and senior research associate at the Institute for Community College Development at Cornell University.

4

Community colleges now depend on fundraising to fill a growing gap between institutional needs and financial support from tuition and government taxes. As a result, fundraising has become a critical component of fiscal leadership. This chapter describes emerging ways in which fundraising is being viewed and organized in the community college.

Leading the Fundraising Effort

G. Jeremiah Ryan, James C. Palmer

Recurring economic recessions, uncertain levels of tax support, and pressing fiscal demands of health care, K–12 education, and corrections have complicated the task of sustaining financial support for community colleges since the early 1970s. Moving beyond traditional lobbying for precarious government appropriations, fiscal leadership now includes fundraising as a complement to institutional planning and prioritization (see Chapter Eight of this volume), the management of restricted government grants (see Chapter Five), and the development of cooperative programs that leverage corporate resources to support workforce development (see Chapter Six). The fundraising component of fiscal leadership has become particularly promising as community colleges gain increased recognition and respect for their essential contributions to educational opportunity and workforce development. Leveraging this increased visibility, community college leaders can expand their institutional revenue base beyond tuition and government tax support.

Not all colleges have the same capacity to invest in fundraising. Large urban or suburban institutions—unlike rural institutions—may have a healthy mix of businesses and industries that rely on the college for worker training and whose executives form an influential corps of community leaders who can lend support to the college's foundation (Ryan, 1989). Yet with the right leadership, all colleges have at least some capacity to secure private funds. Success depends on the extent to which fundraising is viewed as part of the institution's overall community relations effort, the ways that fundraising tasks are assigned and coordinated, and the strategies used to ensure returns on investment in fundraising campaigns.

NEW DIRECTIONS FOR COMMUNITY COLLEGES, no. 132, Winter 2005 © Wiley Periodicals, Inc

Taking a Broad View of Fundraising

Fundraising at community colleges has evolved from a peripheral activity facilitating occasional donations for scholarship or equipment funds to a strategic effort that seeks resources through mutually supportive relations between the institution and its external constituencies (Bass, 2003; Hall, 2002; Wenrich and Reid, 2003). Often these supportive relations are forged by college foundations, which are nonprofit "incorporated 501(c)(3) organizations [that] exist to raise and manage private resources supporting the mission and priorities of" the institution (Association of Governing Boards and Council for the Advancement and Support of Education, 2005, n.p.). Governed by their own boards, college-affiliated foundations "have a decided advantage over public institutions undertaking the management of funds and endowments," because they are freer to "assume a risk level greater than that permitted by the constraints placed on governing boards" (Phelan, 1997, p. 10). Just as importantly, they involve influential citizens "in enhancing the quality of the institution and supporting its future" (p. 7).

An example of a successful community college and foundation relationship can be found in the Rising Star program at the Dallas County Community College District, which provides scholarships of approximately $2,000 to economically disadvantaged students from Dallas County who earned a B average or better in high school, graduated in the top 40 percent of their high school graduating class, or scored at a certain level of the Texas assessment skills program (Whiston, 2002). Funds for the program were collected from area businesses in an effort led by the chairman of the Dallas County Community College Foundation board. In effect, the foundation became a broker between the district and business and civic communities, facilitating a program that furthers both the district's goal of providing educational access and the larger community's need for an educated workforce (Whiston, 2002; Wenrich and Reid, 2003).

A broad view of fundraising thus involves more than publicity or convincing others to donate to a worthy cause. Instead, it builds naturally on the community college's traditional responsiveness to local service districts, and secures resources through *exchange relationships* and *communal relationships* with key constituencies. Drawing on the work of Huang (1997), Hall (2002) explains that exchange relationships entail the exchange of expertise or resources, as in the case of a corporation that donates technical equipment to a college that provides customized training for its employees. Communal relationships are more a function of mutual commitment, in which "the college and its publics support each other because each wants the other to thrive, regardless of any short-term benefit received" (Hall, 2002, p. 57). Examples include donations that are made by area citizens or corporations who view the college as an essential contributor to the overall well-being of the community. Hall suggests that although college partnerships may begin as exchange relationships, college leaders can "provide a vision of a more communal goal," perhaps "moving the relationship to a more philanthropic outcome in the future that will benefit the donor, the college, and the community" (p. 58).

Presidential leadership is essential to the establishment of these relationships. After all, the president articulates the institution's mission (Vaughan, 1989) and is the college's "living logo" (McGee, 2003, p. 46). If colleges are to realize the full potential of their community relationships, the president must be willing to devote a great deal of his or her time—much of it off campus—to developing and sustaining these relations. Although some of this time will be devoted to soliciting gifts, the president should seek out capable and influential community leaders for membership on the foundation board. In addition, he or she should remain active in the community by becoming involved on the boards of area nonprofit agencies and otherwise honing networks that will increase the visibility of the college and identify possibilities for mutual action between the college and key constituencies. This external work may be viewed unfavorably by some faculty and staff members, and perhaps even by some trustees, who expect the president to devote more time to internal, academic matters. But this traditional, academic view of presidential leadership must give way to a new, outward-looking paradigm if colleges are to substantially increase revenue streams beyond tuition and government tax allocations.

Organizing the Fundraising Effort

Of course, the president cannot raise funds alone. A professional fundraising staff reporting directly to the president or to a chief advancement officer (who has overall responsibility for fundraising and reports to the president) is essential. Working in tandem with the college foundation, this staff can seek out possible funding sources, conduct background research that prepares the president (and others) to make the institution's case to potential donors, and help develop possible funding opportunities that emerge through the college's community relationships. Because most community college development offices will have only one or two staff members, the president must hire development professionals who, in addition to working effectively with external constituencies, have the capacity to engage faculty, staff, and other members of the college community in the institution's fundraising efforts. In the long run, fundraising will be successful to the extent that it is viewed "more as a process than a structure, one that builds upon relationships and is embedded in the whole organization" (Jackson and Keener, 2002, p. 3).

The president's job is to coordinate the work of those involved in fundraising and to ensure that they present a unified message and image to external constituencies. Community college presidents can facilitate this coordination by placing the development office in a larger institutional advancement division that includes public relations, grants management, planning, and other offices that connect the college with external stake-holders. Involving development staff in strategic planning efforts is partic-ularly important, and reduces the risk of "soliciting and accepting gifts that shift priorities and siphon resources from high priority subjects to lower priority ones" (Hall, 2002, p. 52). In addition, including development staff in planning can help ensure that the college's strategic plan addresses fund-raising as an important priority and provides "a road map for soliciting external funds" (Glass and Jackson, 1998, p. 725).

Steps can also be taken to ensure coordination between the college's development office and the college foundation. Regular communication between these two entities should be encouraged so that respective donors do not receive duplicate requests for funding (Herbkersman and Hibbert-Jones, 2003). In addition, the president should negotiate a memorandum of understanding between the foundation board and the college's trustees, affirming the primacy of the latter in determining fundraising priorities and spelling out the respective roles of the college on the one hand and the foun-dation on the other. For example, a 2002 memorandum of understanding struck between the Palomar Community College District and the Palomar College Foundation specifies that whereas the foundation will "conduct all activities . . . relative to securing, maintaining, and increasing scholarship funds," the district will have responsibility for "selecting recipients accord-ing to donor criteria" (Palomar Community College District, 2002, n.p.). In addition, the Association of Governing Boards and the Council for the Advancement and Support of Education (2005), which have collaborated on the development of an online "illustrative memorandum of understanding," note that these memoranda should, among other features, "clarify the foun-dation's standing as an independent public trust," describe "how funds shall be transferred between the foundation and the institution," and detail poli-cies concerning the "use and sharing [of] donor and alumni records" (n.p.).

Securing a Return on Investment

Once a community college's fundraising effort is in place, strategies must be developed to ensure a maximum return on the institutional investment required to sustain that effort. The pressure to demonstrate the benefits of a fundraising program will be high, because it is unlikely that the college will raise enough unrestricted cash to subsidize the development office completely. Most gifts received in a fundraising campaign are restricted to specific purposes, and it is important for the college to show early and sub-stantial success in securing restricted gifts that yield highly visible benefits to the college. In a case study of the inception of a community college foun-dation in North Carolina, Jenkins and Glass (1999) found that the early receipt of large gifts that "served as a major source of student financial aid" were essential to the success of the foundation (p. 605).

One strategy for securing early returns on investment is to concentrate initially on well-established community partnerships. Reaching out to alumni may pay off in the long run, but more immediate results can be obtained by concentrating early efforts on corporate and business partners that have long been involved in the college's workforce development mission. This is especially true if strong personal ties exist between local corporate executives and the college's president, trustees, or foundation board members. In rural areas with a weaker business or industrial presence, retirees who have taken noncredit, community education courses and who see the college as an important cultural resource may be a promising starting point for the fundraising effort (Bass, 2003).

Another strategy is to look for leveraging opportunities in which securing one source of funding leads naturally to another. In some cases, private funds can be secured in the wake of public grants. Brumbach and Villadsen (2002) offer an example from Brookhaven College (Texas). Responding to a company that expressed interest in relocating to the college's district, the college secured state funding to train the company's workers. This was followed by "a significant donation for a new program providing scholarships to area high school students and a . . . program specifically targeted to the new industry" (pp. 83–84). These contributions were driven by the college's attention to a shared community concern for economic and workforce development. Rather than asking for funds to support the college's day-to-day operations, Brookhaven appealed to the concerns of public agencies and private benefactors. As Brumbach and Villadsen explain, "The task for the resource development operation is to ferret out those elements of the college's goals and needs that can be incorporated into public funding agency requests for proposals or will fulfill the interest of a potential donor" (p. 80).

Conclusion

Although community colleges are, in comparison to four-year institutions, relative newcomers to fundraising, their close ties to area businesses and citizens offer promising opportunities to secure private funds. Presidential efforts to organize fundraising campaigns that capitalize on these ties will become increasingly important as diminished state support leads to ever-rising tuition rates, which may pose a threat to student access. At some point, college leaders can no longer say, "We have no choice but to raise tuition." Our commitment to students requires increased attention to the development of alternative revenue streams, and private fundraising is the most logical place to start.

References

Association of Governing Boards and the Council for the Advancement and Support of Education. "AGB-CASE Illustrative Memorandum of Understanding Between a Foundation and Host Institution or System." Washington, D.C.: Association of Governing Boards and the Council for the Advancement and Support of Education, 2005. http://www.case.org/Content/AboutCASE/Display.cfm?CONTAINERID=40&CONTENTITEMID=5023&CRUMB=3. Accessed Aug. 8, 2005.

Bass, D. "From the Foundations Up: Contexts for Change in Community College Advancement." In M. D. Milliron, G. E. de los Santos, and B. Browning (eds.), *Successful Approaches to Fundraising and Development.* New Directions for Community Colleges, no. 124. San Francisco: Jossey-Bass, 2003.

Brumbach, M. A., and Villadsen, A. W. "At the Edge of Chaos: The Essentials of Resource Development for the Community's College." *Community College Journal of Research and Practice,* 2002, 26(1), 77–86.

Glass, J. C., Jr., and Jackson, K. L. "Integrating Resource Development and Institutional Planning." *Community College Journal of Research and Practice,* 1998, 22(8), 715–740.

Hall, M. R. "Building on Relationships: A Fundraising Approach for Community Colleges." *Community College Journal of Research and Practice,* 2002, 26(1), 47–60.

Herbkersman, N., and Hibbert-Jones, K. "Grants Development in Community Colleges." In M. D. Milliron, G. E. de los Santos, and B. Browning (eds.), *Successful Approaches to Fundraising and Development.* New Directions for Community Colleges, no. 124. San Francisco: Jossey-Bass, 2003.

Huang, Y. H. "Public Relations Strategies, Relational Outcomes, and Conflict Management Strategies." Unpublished doctoral dissertation, University of Maryland, College Park, 1997.

Jackson, K. L., and Keener, B. J. "Introduction to Community College Resource Development: Creating Preferred Futures." *Community College Journal of Research and Practice,* 2002, 26(1), 1–6.

Jenkins, L. W., and Glass, J. C., Jr. "Inception, Growth, and Development of a Community College Foundation: Lessons to Be Learned." *Community College Journal of Research and Practice,* 1999, 23(6), 593–612.

McGee, E. A. "The Role of the President in Supporting the College's Foundation." In M. D. Milliron, G. E. de los Santos, and B. Browning (eds.), *Successful Approaches to Fundraising and Development.* New Directions for Community Colleges, no. 124. San Francisco: Jossey-Bass, 2003.

Palomar Community College District. "Governing Board Minutes." Apr. 9, 2002. http://www.palomar.edu/GB/2002/040902_Board_Min.pdf. Accessed July 20, 2005.

Phelan, J. F. "The Changing Case for Establishing College and University Foundations." In J. F. Phelan (ed.), *College and University Foundations: Serving America's Public Higher Education.* Washington, D.C.: Association of Governing Boards of Universities and Colleges, 1997. (ED 406 925)

Ryan, G. J. (ed.). *Initiating a Fund-Raising Program: A Model for the Community College.* Washington, D.C.: Council for the Advancement and Support of Education, 1989.

Vaughan, G. B. *Leadership in Transition: The Community College Presidency.* New York: American Council on Education and Macmillan, 1989.

Wenrich, J. W., and Reid, B. L. "It's Not the Race I Signed Up For, But It's the Race I'm In: The Role of Community College Presidents." In M. D. Milliron, G. E. de los Santos, and B. Browning (eds.), *Successful Approaches to Fundraising and Development.* New Directions for Community Colleges, no. 124. San Francisco: Jossey-Bass, 2003.

Whiston, K. "Rising Star Raises Success." *Community College Journal of Research and Practice,* 2002, 26(10), 787–791.

G. JEREMIAH RYAN *is president of Raritan Valley Community College in North Branch, New Jersey.*

JAMES C. PALMER *is professor of educational administration and foundations at Illinois State University.*

5

Workforce development grants and contracts are important methods for sustaining financial support for community colleges. This chapter details decision factors, college issues, possible pitfalls, and methods for procuring and handling government contracts and grants for workforce training.

Sustaining Financial Support Through Workforce Development Grants and Contracts

Mary A. Brumbach

The call comes. It could be the mayor, the head of the chamber of commerce, the president of the local workforce board, a consultant, or the director of economic development for the city. It may be an early alert that a local company is facing closure because workers are unable to meet new demands for skills, or that a consortium of hospitals or small businesses is trying to fill skilled employee shortages. These scenarios represent opportunities and challenges for any community college interested in fostering local economic development, training employees, and garnering the resources to support those efforts.

Securing government-sponsored grants—targeted grants that assist local employers in workforce training or retraining—has become an important way of funding the community college's growing workforce development role. In fact, community college participation in grant-funded workforce development programs is in some ways a marriage of necessity driven by state and employer needs to provide workforce training. However, this marriage also benefits the community college. Tuition revenues for trainee classes, and where applicable, state reimbursements for technical education, can add to the institution's financial resources. In addition, these grants bolster the community college's long-established role of offering training incentives to attract relocating companies and encourage existing companies to stay in the local area (Batt and Osterman, 1993).

Managing grants and contracts requires considerable resources and staff time. Therefore, colleges need to carefully consider what will be required in

NEW DIRECTIONS FOR COMMUNITY COLLEGES, no. 132, Winter 2005 © Wiley Periodicals, Inc.

planning the incorporation of grants and contracts into the mix of institutional fiscal support. Drawing on experiences at Brookhaven College (Texas), this chapter discusses challenges that the management of these grants poses for college administrators, key questions that administrators must consider as they plan their involvement in grant-funded workforce development programs, and the tasks involved in planning grant proposals.

Brookhaven College

Brookhaven College is a suburban institution located on the outskirts of Dallas and is one of the seven Dallas County Community Colleges. Brookhaven has approximately 10,500 credit students and an additional 8,000 continuing education students, and has been growing rapidly in the past five years. It is a comprehensive institution, offering a full complement of transfer academic programs, student support services, and technical or occupational programs. The college is home to the unique Ellison Miles Geotechnology Institute, which was created in 2000 by a $3.5 million gift that provided corporate-level training space for the earth sciences industry professionals, K–12 teacher outreach, and public awareness of geoscience issues. Brookhaven has become a significant "technology transfer" institution linking industry, educators, and students.

When the Texas legislature created its Skills Development Fund in 1996, Brookhaven College was one of the first in the state to receive an award. These new funds were created to link business and industry with the training capabilities of community colleges while permitting colleges to increase capacity for such training. Brookhaven has received eight grants in the past eight years totaling more than $4 million and providing training to over two thousand individuals in companies in the financial services, electronics manufacturing, managerial, and customer service industries. As a result, the college has become a significant partner in efforts to attract businesses to its service area. Among the most successful relationships was the relocation of several of JPMorgan Chase's business units to the community. The availability of training funds was a key factor in the international banking and financial services firm's decision to move these operations to Texas. Because Texas funds continuing education and vocational training in the same manner as credit training, the Skills Development Fund grant also included over $4 million in revenue for corporate and continuing education.

The two grants received in partnership with JPMorgan have had numerous dividends, including a stronger working relationship with the city, recognition of the college's role in attracting a new business sector with thirty-six hundred high-paying positions and construction of major new buildings in the area, and additional nonfunded contracts for training JPMorgan employees. As an added bonus, the company has contributed to scholarship funds at the system and college level and donates computers and other equipment on a regular basis. Through its extensive experience with workforce training grants, Brookhaven has become more sophisticated in its ability to monitor training participants, identify and hire industry-qualified instructors, and provide responsive service to a wide variety of clients. These skills are imperative, because each year the funding process becomes more complex, as do the accountability and regulatory measures.

Challenges and Benefits of Managing Government Grants and Contracts

There are many challenges inherent in managing workforce development grants and contracts. Government funding requires speed, customization, and measurable outcomes, demands that may run counter to a community college's routine disciplinary course offerings and relatively limited schedule variations. In addition, funds for workforce development usually arrive with numerous strings attached. There are often stringent requirements for participant eligibility, numerous demands for employer support, including training time and compensation, and agreements to raise workers' salaries upon successful completion of training. In addition, these opportunities require extensive disclosure of business plans and employee policies, and are frequently reliant on cost reimbursement when trainees have met specified outcomes for course completion and skills attainment. In this age of accountability, colleges must also comply with significant tracking and reporting of individual placement outcomes, including starting and ending salaries and long-term retention (between ninety days and a year) at the company or in similar jobs. In some instances, such as with the individual training accounts offered as part of the Workforce Investment Act (WIA), when a college accepts one student into a program, it is then required to track every student in the program, whether or not the student is funded by the workforce board. Failure to meet targets or verify results can mean a 25 percent or greater reduction in anticipated funding.

These requirements can be especially challenging because participants in workforce training programs are often in lower-skilled jobs, have not yet experienced formal training, and in the case of those being funded through such sources as Temporary Assistance for Needy Families (TANF), often have child care needs and family expectations. Community colleges must provide case managers to maintain contact, ensure retention in the program through completion, and resolve problems for these students. Workers who were laid off or are being retrained under the Trade Adjustment Act have similar needs, and case workers must also deal with the emotional and psychological effects of job losses and changed life circumstances on long-term employees.

Despite these challenges, there are many benefits for community colleges that become involved in managing workforce development grants and contracts. First, these programs allow colleges to tap local, state, and federal government resources to provide training programs for new hires and incumbent workers. These funds support economic development, assist in employer retention and relocation, and help raise the quality of life in a college's service area. Government grants and contracts can also yield additional funding for other programs and college needs, because they often result in an increased number of students eligible for Pell grants, donations for scholarships, gifts of equipment, and an increased willingness among business leaders to serve on college advisory committees. These grants can also help initiate new programs, draw new students and their families to the college, and reap goodwill and approval for the college among local taxpayers. Therefore, when a community college is considering entering into workforce development grants or contracts, it must always weigh the burdens and reporting requirements against potential long-term benefits to the college.

Preparing for Government Grants and Contracts

Before committing to seek government funding for workforce development, community colleges must ask and answer several questions.

Does Workforce Training Fall Within the College's Existing Capabilities? This question is best answered by examining the college's continuing education function, the mission under which most workforce training is delivered. To participate in workforce training opportunities, community colleges must find instructors with industry credentials, provide instruction on the employer's site or in college facilities, and have the ability to procure needed teaching materials—including entire curricula—in a specific industry, such as regulatory training for health care providers. Except in instances of significant customization, most training must be done at "off-the-shelf" prices (in other words, at the same cost as published in college schedules). Therefore, proposals for workforce development grants or contracts must demonstrate efficiency and price competitiveness. These opportunities sometimes require community colleges to provide training in proprietary software, such as that used in financial institutions or in companies providing technical assistance or maintaining and troubleshooting computer software and hardware. Sometimes, because of issues of confidentiality, community colleges must use external computer drives when working with a company's materials, a practice that adds time and complexity to workforce training if it is conducted on the college campus. In contrast, if training is held on-site at a company, college instructors must be able to pass security screenings in order to teach in secured areas of the complex and have access to propriety material. Community colleges must consider all of these issues when deciding whether workforce development grants and contracts fall within their existing capabilities.

Brookhaven College has relied heavily on its contacts in the city and business community to determine if a particular grant possibility is feasible. Take, for example, a recent opportunity that emerged through the Ellison

Miles Geotechnology Institute. An international oil services company that trained operators in the area but placed them overseas came to the college seeking to partner on a Skills Development Fund grant. Although the training would have used a combination of college and company expertise (their instructors would be certified as meeting college standards), the outcomes did not match the requirements for a new and expanding company in Texas, and both parties decided not to pursue the grant.

Does the College Have the Facilities and Technological Resources Available to Provide Training on Campus? Answering this question entails careful consideration of how well a workforce training program would fit with other college initiatives. Training in software and soft skills such as teamwork, time management, supervision, and productivity is easier to run using existing facilities and technological resources than specialized work in manufacturing (for example, work with geographic information systems or clean rooms for semiconductor chip manufacturing companies). Each of these specialized areas can require significant investments in the facility, software, and equipment and must, therefore, have long-term potential if the college is to make a financial commitment. If short-term training is required, most likely the company will have to provide training space and equipment. However, if community colleges want to compete for long-term workforce development grants and contracts, they might consider making a significant investment in training facilities and equipment. By leveraging a significant capital investment, community colleges can often secure equipment donations and gifts for other college purposes from industries that will benefit from the new facilities (Brumbach and McGee, 1995).

Will the Training Enhance Current College Offerings? Community colleges contemplating workforce training must ask whether an opportunity will enhance current offerings or fall into an area in which the institution wants to build capacity. With its launch of new programs in allied health and nursing, Brookhaven has been actively seeking partners to enhance continuing education offerings in the health care arena and has submitted grant proposals designed to accomplish that outcome. As well, the college is currently focusing its grant-seeking efforts on securing funding to complement private donations supporting a recently approved program in geospatial technologies.

Is the College Prepared to Comply with Stringent Requirements Imposed by the Funding Agency? Complying with stringent agency requirements can be burdensome if colleges do not understand them well and do not put processes into place early. Colleges that are familiar with more traditional modes of funding may have difficulty documenting the time and effort spent by grant-funded personnel. Because most workforce development efforts are funded through governmental agencies, community colleges must aggressively keep records, track participants, and report hours (kept in daily logs) on a monthly basis. They must pay particular attention to regulations on the subcontracting of services or the designation of subrecipients as defined by the agencies. A subrecipient is generally a partner in the application; a subcontractor is selected based on competitive review of pricing and ability to provide services. Finally, community colleges—especially those new to grant funding—must carefully review contract stipulations and work closely with agency program directors.

From an organizational perspective, it is helpful to have staff with expertise in interpreting regulations and managing complex participant databases. Manuals for many workforce funding agencies exceed two hundred pages and have numerous finite regulations. The bureaucracy that surrounds such funds can be daunting, and the staff member in charge must be persistent and positive. In addition, to claim money from the funding agency, invoices must usually be processed on a monthly or quarterly basis. These invoices, prepared by the project manager, require documentation that includes the number of hours each participant spent in training, benchmarks achieved, and any other measures included in the contract. Because such detail must frequently be supplied by the company for which training is being conducted, agreeing early on whether to use identification numbers or Social Security numbers, how demographic data on participants will be gathered, and the person who will act as the college's primary point of contact will eliminate unnecessary delays. Generally, the college and company create a memorandum of understanding that covers both entities' responsibilities in the implementation of the contract.

Can Noncredit Workforce Training Courses Be Converted to Credit If the Student So Chooses? In some instances trainees will begin in grant-funded continuing education courses and find that they have both the ability and the motivation to work toward a college degree. Therefore, it is important to have mechanisms in place that allow students to provide evidence, through testing or portfolio reviews, that they have acquired knowledge and skills equivalent to those gained in credit courses. Assessment mechanisms help students complete their degrees and serve as a bridge between the college's credit programs and the noncredit training that grant-funded workforce development programs often provide.

Will College Faculty and Staff Welcome Program Participants or See Them as Intrusive? Training program participants are legitimate community college students. TANF and WIA clients have many of the same characteristics as first-generation community college students. Others, especially those being retrained, may already hold college degrees. In all cases, workforce training students and their families are both current and potential students, and colleges would be well served to view their introduction to workforce training participants as a long-range recruiting opportunity. At Brookhaven, approximately 25 percent of students enrolling in workforce training or continuing education programs eventually pursue credit offerings.

The degree of students' involvement with the college will be determined by the location of their training. If the training is delivered on campus, participants may take advantage of the wide variety of college services available to continuing education students. Case managers may use college support services to help refer TANF and WIA clients to health and welfare programs, on-campus groups, and other community-based organizations. However, when training is offered off campus, the college will need to make a special effort to link participants to the institution through financial aid seminars, information about on-campus events, and possibly seminars on career directions and résumé writing.

If these and similar efforts are not made, workforce training students can be seen by some, such as faculty in the academic transfer program, as an intrusion on the college's main mission. College leaders can make a compelling case for embracing workforce training clientele by noting that the college is providing opportunities that would otherwise be unavailable to the very students that community colleges were designed to reach. Institutional leaders will have to reinforce to college constituents that workforce training efforts meet community needs and generate revenue that remains at the local campus.

Can the College Meet the Project's Time Lines, and Are Staff Available to Manage the Project? In today's globally competitive economy, community colleges have very short time frames in which to respond to pending announcements of plant relocations, closures, or major layoffs. Furthermore, because corporations often determine sites for new plants using the Internet and make few public announcements before determining new sites, community colleges must be ready to jump on opportunities when they arise. To meet the much faster pace of corporate decision making, community colleges interested in pursuing government-funded workforce training grants and contracts must have a flexible and comprehensive infrastructure designed to respond rapidly to opportunities, prepare proposals, deliver training in a timely fashion, and provide grant management services.

Community colleges must create an infrastructure that allows for rapid response across both operational and instructional territories. First, colleges should appoint a single point of contact for managing workforce training contracts. This person should be capable of managing the college's response to partnering and proposal opportunities and able to collaborate with faculty and staff in continuing education divisions and the business office, proposal writers, and individuals skilled in interpretation and implementation of extensive contract requirements. The contact person should also obtain the informed consent of the college governance team. He or she should have equal footing with other vice presidents and should be given a title similar to chief resource development officer. This person should have a portfolio that includes economic development and environmental scanning, in addition to experience in public and private fundraising.

Brookhaven College takes a nontraditional approach to responding to business and industry training needs, particularly when funded by a third party such as the state. When an opportunity becomes available, the vice president of resource and economic development quickly assembles an ad hoc team that includes the grant specialist, deans of the involved divisions, the dean of corporate and continuing education, and likely, the dean who coordinates new program development. If there are student issues that need to be addressed in the participant population, appropriate people from student services will be included. An initial meeting covers feasibility, impact on facilities, short- and long-term impacts and benefits, the availability of training resources including the need to acquire them, and the time line. The team decides whether to continue exploration, arrange meetings with the principals from the industries, and prepare preliminary documentation or decline the opportunity.

Once initial exploration of the opportunity is completed, the vice president briefs the cabinet and begins the proposal development process. Ad hoc team members are kept informed via e-mail or quick update meetings. This approach, described as an "adhocracy," a method often used in rapid response industries, permits great flexibility in meeting demands without creating self-perpetuating personnel-heavy organizations. Teams of individuals form to meet a specific need and then dissolve when the development process concludes and implementation begins (Brumbach, 2002; Brumbach and Villadsen, 2002). College leaders can orient operational units to the special demands of such funding ahead of time, and by reinforcing the college's commitment to workforce education (perhaps by emphasizing the "community" in the college's name), the president can help create a foundation for saying yes when the needs arise.

Bringing workforce training grants under one umbrella unit that can tap expertise in other sectors of the college on a just-in-time basis has proven to be an effective strategy at Brookhaven College. It allows highly specialized personnel to manage complex contracts with varied requirements for documentation, with support from those who have expertise in credit and continuing education curriculum requirements, labor market information, and instructional design.

Applying for Government Grants and Contracts

If, after carefully considering the preceding questions, the college decides to secure fiscal support for workforce development through grants and contracts, a significant up-front investment must be made to seek out and compete for these grants. Sources of funding for workforce training vary by state and location. Whether from the Department of Labor, the state workforce commission, or the local workforce board, funding is usually targeted toward special-needs populations, dislocated workers, incumbent workers, or companies relocating or expanding operations. Those preparing the proposal will rely heavily on local employment data and forecasted needs, as well as demographic information. The constant monitoring of external data should be the responsibility of the workforce development team rather than institutional researchers, who are primarily focused on internal data and required reports.

To be competitive, a college will need to have completed some preliminary research in local needs and trends and have comparative market information on the costs of its offerings versus others available in the area. Identifying assets that can be used for training is a worthwhile exercise; colleges that have high-quality training facilities are often able to submit a competitively priced proposal because they do not have to rent facilities.

Company information required in grant proposals ranges from employee benefit plans and nondiscrimination policies to current salary levels by classification. In today's competitive market, many businesses will decline a workforce training opportunity because all this information will become public record. Data on the numbers of potential participants meeting funding guidelines will require extensive research on census data as well as information on transportation possibilities and realistic assessments of the likelihood of participants' success. Targets set by local workforce boards for successful retention through training and placement are, in some cases, as high as 85 percent. For some populations with economic and educational disadvantages, however, that benchmark in unattainable. If the funding package is to produce new hires from a pool of applicants, many colleges recruit more students than required because dropout rates can be high. Establishing relationships with community and faith-based groups that can refer potential participants is valuable, and it does not hurt to include them in the recruitment portion of the project.

Funding for workforce development grants is generally limited to a per-person cost multiplied by the number of participants. In most instances, books and supplies are factored into the average cost per trainee, and a direct administrative allowance in the range of 10 to 15 percent can be used to cover the cost of managing the contract. Grants may or may not include an allowance to cover the cost of rented facilities. In addition, for most workforce grants, community colleges can either ask for funding to cover an instructor's salary or request tuition (which is then used to defray the cost of an instructor). Generally, if a college requests money to pay an instructor, it cannot also charge tuition. Brookhaven College most often requests tuition.

Conclusion

So, the call comes. A new company with high-paying jobs is scouting locations and the mayor wants to know what the college has to offer in terms of training and access to training funds. The college team is called together. In short order, the team determines that this opportunity fits local, state, and regional needs for which funding is available. In addition, the team determines that it is well within the college's mission and capacity to deliver this training, or that it will strengthen an existing program. The college is aware of the challenges inherent in competing for and securing government funding for workforce training, but knows also the return on investment it can expect from workforce training grants: increased enrollment, additional resources for training and student needs, and an enhanced role in the community.

References

Batt, R., and Osterman, P. *A National Policy for Workplace Training: Lessons from State and Local Experiences.* Working paper no. 106. Washington, D.C.: Economic Policy Institute, 1993.

Brumbach, M. "Adapting Growth Policy to Community College Development." *Community College Journal,* 2002, 72(4), 16–19.

Brumbach, M., and McGee, A. "Leveraged Investments: Corporations + Community Colleges." *Community College Journal,* 1995, 65(7), 22–27.

Brumbach, M., and Villadsen, A. "At the Edge of Chaos: The Essentials of Resource Development for the Community's College." *Community College Journal of Research and Practice,* 2002, 26(1), 77–86.

MARY A. BRUMBACH is vice president of resource and economic development at Brookhaven College of the Dallas County Community College District.

6

This chapter describes the joint associate degree program between Illinois Central College and Caterpillar, Inc., and discusses how collaborative instructional programs can help sustain financial support for community colleges.

Caterpillar Inc.'s Think Big Program at Illinois Central College: Sustaining Financial Support Through Collaborative Partnerships

John Stuart Erwin

Community colleges have an obligation to train workers for local industries and businesses. The training mandate is embedded in the core mission and foundational purpose of community colleges and is based on a close understanding of local community educational needs. However, colleges by themselves do not always have the resources or expertise needed to create curricula that are tightly aligned with the workplace. Thus, to sustain financial support for meaningful workforce development, community colleges must examine alternative and innovative program designs.

Cooperative educational programs, which recast curricula as joint endeavors of both colleges and employers, have emerged as one way to secure funds for workforce development. This chapter describes one such endeavor undertaken by Illinois Central College (ICC), a public community college in East Peoria, Illinois, that enrolls thirteen thousand students, and Caterpillar, Inc., a Fortune 100 company and the world's largest manufacturer of earth-moving equipment. Pooling financial and physical resources as well as instructional expertise, ICC and Caterpillar implemented an associate degree program that prepares repair technicians for Caterpillar dealerships. Begun in 1999, the "Think Big" program now enrolls forty-eight full-time students (and has a waiting list of three hundred), each sponsored by local Caterpillar dealerships. Each semester these students undergo eight weeks of on-campus instruction at a Caterpillar-financed facility on ICC's campus, then participate in an eight-week paid internship at one of Caterpillar's local dealerships. After two years of instruction and internships, students in this program graduate with associate of applied science degrees and as dealer technicians for Caterpillar equipment. Twenty-four students graduate from the program each year.

The Think Big program at Illinois Central College, the first of its kind, serves as a prototype for dealer service technician programs at Caterpillar. The program trains students to service or promote Caterpillar machines using cutting-edge diagnostic and maintenance systems, advanced technologies, and high-tech tools. Since its inception at Illinois Central College, thirteen other colleges in nine states (California, Oklahoma, North Dakota, Ohio, South Carolina, Missouri, Arizona, Georgia, and Texas) and four other countries (Canada, Chile, Peru, and Ecuador) have joined Caterpillar's Think Big program. Europe is currently considering joining Caterpillar's Think Big instructional model as well (J. Schmidt, personal communication, Oct. 2004).

The following pages describe ICC's experience with Think Big, noting its origins, the ways it is funded, and its curricular design. The chapter also describes how students are recruited, the role Caterpillar dealerships play in their education, and the student outcomes that have been achieved to date. After summarizing the benefits of the program to the college and its corporate partner, the chapter concludes with a discussion of the factors that contributed to the program's successful implementation.

Origins of the Program

The first step in creating a successful collaboration between a community college and a private business is a needs assessment that reflects the community's demand for a given curriculum. In 1998, Caterpillar, Inc., initiated discussions with Illinois Central College about the potential for a dealership technician training program. According to Jerry Wright (personal communication, Jan. 2005), a trustee of Illinois Central College, top executives at Caterpillar had met with dealers throughout the country and had examined data projections that indicated a severe shortage of dealer technicians over the next five years. Dealers were concerned that there simply were not enough trained people to assume these jobs. Caterpillar understood that with fewer trained dealer technicians, equipment sales and service could falter. Company executives also knew that because an apprenticeship program did not exist, they must create a pathway to address a void in trained technicians. Caterpillar's corporate offices had not previously trained its dealerships' technicians, but as they thought more about the potential crisis, Caterpillar executives decided to invest in academic programs at local community colleges to educate dealer technicians (J. Wright, personal communication, Jan. 2005). In their eyes, this investment would ensure excellent service for Caterpillar's customers and would provide dealerships with skilled employees who knew the intricacies of Caterpillar's new machines. This program would also benefit the community college by helping it meet the training needs of a global corporation whose world headquarters resides in the heart of the college district.

Funding the Program

Caterpillar initially allocated $5 million to this technician training and educational program. Almost half of this money, $2 million, was used for curriculum design and marketing. Another $1.5 million went to Illinois Central College to build the training facility, which houses two computerized classrooms, a tool room, offices, a shop area large enough to store a variety of test equipment and tear-down engines, and bays where students can work on machines of all sizes. Caterpillar also uses the campus facility to host visitors from other states and countries who wish to view the Think Big program. The remaining $1.5 million was used to procure equipment and defray miscellaneous expenses. For example, Caterpillar gives over $5,000 each year to pay for program incidentals such as tools, worktables, and diagnostic equipment. Caterpillar has also donated up-to-date large tractor equipment that the community college could not possibly purchase on its limited budget. Although neither the state of Illinois nor the Illinois Community College Board contributed hard money to this project, Illinois Central College dedicated land for the training facility, provided administrative oversight for curriculum development, hired the two full-time instructors, and coordinates student recruitment, selection, and graduation processes.

Curriculum Development

Caterpillar developed the curriculum based on previous dealer technician apprenticeship programs, and ICC's curriculum committee approved the courses and degree requirements. The curriculum emphasizes hands-on work and close collaboration with Caterpillar and its dealerships. Students spend half of each sixteen-week semester at Illinois Central College doing hands-on training in laboratories and learning from curriculum modules in the classroom. The learning modules are divided by themes relevant to the equipment. For example, one module is on transmissions, another is on the electronics that operate Caterpillar machinery. During these eight weeks, instructors impart to students a set of objectives that have proven to be key to this work-based learning collaborative (Wolff and Copa, 2003).

During the second eight weeks, students intern at a local Caterpillar dealership and work with a mentor who monitors how they perform in the work environment. This curriculum design allows students to reinforce their learning at both the theoretical and applied levels. In addition, by observing how students transfer their knowledge from the classroom to the work world, dealership managers can assess students' knowledge and potential effectiveness as employees. Think Big's curriculum is effective because it combines classroom learning with real world experience at a dealership. Because the community college, the dealerships, and Caterpillar, Inc., were all involved in designing the curriculum, planners from all three parties were able to ensure that workforce needs were met and that students were adequately prepared for employment.

Two significant challenges surfaced during the development of the program, however. First, ICC had to reconfigure its academic calendar for students in the program, moving from a sixteen-week to an eight-week curriculum. In addition, the college had to integrate the physical science requirements for the degree into instructional modules in program courses. For example, Caterpillar wanted heat and hydraulics to be taught as modules in an eight-week course on engine design. Therefore, the mechanics of physics needed to be taught on a just-in-time basis so that students could immediately apply engine design theory to practice. In a traditional curriculum, ICC would have required students to take a separate physical science course in a sixteen-week semester. Now the dealership technician students meet the physical science requirement at the same time they learn engine design.

Student Recruitment and Selection

Each year, two hundred applicants vie for one of twenty-four seats in the Caterpillar program at ICC. Upon applying to the program, they are invited to the college for an interview and a campus tour. If they wish to participate in the program, during their second visit they are given a series of tests in mathematics, reading comprehension, and English, as well as a mechanical aptitude examination. If students meet the minimum requirements for each of these examinations they are notified and then asked to rank their three top choices of Caterpillar dealerships at which to intern. Students first interview at their first-choice dealership, whose managers determine if the student is the kind of employee they are looking for. If students' first-choice dealership does not select them, they interview at their second choice, and so on. If candidates are not sponsored by any of the first three dealerships, they are not admitted to the program.

Dealership Involvement

When a dealership decides to sponsor a student, it agrees to pay the student $10 per hour. Because students work forty hours per week, their salary totals $3,200 for the eight-week period, enough to pay for tuition and living expenses. Initially, the dealerships balked at paying the student interns, believing they would lose money by compensating students who were not yet able to work at 100 percent capacity. However, Caterpillar and Illinois

Central College illustrated to the dealers that it is financially beneficial to pay the students an hourly wage; it not only helps motivate the interns but also is profitable for the dealers, because they charge $55 an hour for service repairs. Even if student interns work at 50 percent capacity because they are new on the job, dealers still make a profit on each hour a student provides repair service. Indeed, many students actually perform at greater than 50 percent capacity. One former Caterpillar manager said, "We found out that the students actually performed at a higher capacity than expected, which increased the profitability for the dealerships. It also pointed to the fact that the students had the latest information about the newest equipment—knowledge that the experienced dealership technician appreciated learning" (J. Wright, personal communication, Jan. 2005).

The dealers also had to factor in the cost of having a mentor for each intern at the dealership. But because the mentors contribute to students' skills and knowledge, they actually enhance the interns' productivity. Each mentor is a current employee who validates students' learning process and the responsibilities they hold during the time they work at the dealership. These mentors also help students learn expected workplace behaviors such as time management, hygiene, and a positive attitude. Each mentor is an experienced dealer technician who has an aptitude to teach. Potential mentors are screened, selected for teaching tendencies, and then trained. Each knows the curriculum the student intern has just completed and can reinforce students' understanding of instructional materials with actual hands-on service repair experience and guidance. In addition, as Mark Matthews, the program's lead instructor, observes, "We bring the mentors to the college to develop their understanding of their responsibility for reinforcing what the students have learned in class" (personal communication, Oct. 2004).

Program Evaluation and Outcomes

During the students' eight-week internships, ICC monitors and evaluates their progress. Students also receive a score on a completion examination that reflects their learning and gives them a measure of their success in comparison to students in similar programs across the globe. Awards are given to the highest-performing students, who are recognized for their scores on a standardized instrument that tests information taught during the two-year course of study.

In addition, college faculty members, Caterpillar, and the dealerships jointly assess and document program outcomes in annual reviews. Since the program's inception, 90 percent of graduates have been placed at Caterpillar dealerships; 83 percent returned to the dealer that sponsored them. The majority of the students who choose not to return to their sponsor either take a job with another dealership or transfer to a four-year institution. Dealerships recognize that graduates of the Think Big program have detailed knowledge of Caterpillar equipment, and upon employment are immediately able to contribute to the success of the dealership. Thus, students' average annual starting salary is $40,000.

Benefits of the Program

Both parties involved in Think Big benefit from the cooperative program, and both have strengthened their respective enterprises. Illinois Central College gained a much-needed instructional facility and added forty-eight additional full-time students each year. The school also gains the prestige that comes from partnering with a Fortune 100 company. In addition to the initial $5 million investment, the partnership with Caterpillar, Inc., has resulted in $2.5 million in cash to Illinois Central College as well as matching and in-kind gifts totaling $1.5 million.

Caterpillar benefits by securing a much-needed pipeline of educated workers who help sell and maintain its equipment. The dealerships gain well-trained employees who have experience at their own shops, and who have learned from seasoned mentors who were able to impart their experience and wisdom to students in the program. The students also prosper; they complete their associate degree and land a well-paying job without incurring financial debt to pay for tuition. Students also gain marketable skills and recognition for their effort. Indeed, global competition exists for students who complete the Think Big program.

Illinois Central College continues to enjoy a close partnership with Caterpillar, Inc. The corporation supports the ICC Foundation's annual Community Celebration, underwrites special events, and seeks training classes from ICC in everything from computer software to curriculum development for training in its security offices.

Keys to Success

Key elements to the success of the Think Big program at Illinois Central College are trust between the collaborating partners, involvement by college leaders and the board of trustees, dealer commitment and involvement, and a standardized curriculum that is adjusted as equipment changes occur. Of these four important elements to the program, Professor Matthews identified dealership commitment as the most important for sustaining the viability of the program: "Without the dealerships accepting the students as interns, purchasing equipment, and agreeing to the mentorship training, we would not have a program today" (personal communication, Jan. 2005).

Replicating an academic program such as this one between ICC and Caterpillar requires cultural flexibility and consistency in curriculum design. These variables have been key to the adoption of the program by other community colleges in the United States and abroad. Language barriers as well as cultural and contextual differences have led to some small changes in the Think Big program in South American countries. For example, not all of the programs can secure needed instructional equipment because of governmental requirements. Yet even though national and local governments have differing bureaucratic requirements for establishing and maintaining educational programs, the Think Big curriculum remains specific and consistent. Because Caterpillar's earth-moving equipment is standardized around the world, the Think Big curriculum is only altered when product changes are introduced. The program's global reach has the added value of introducing students to the workings of an international organization, even though they secure employment at local dealerships.

Caterpillar and Illinois Central College's dealership technician associate degree program can be replicated at other community colleges if there are adequate resources and a trusting instructional collaboration between partners. College administrators who cultivate relationships built on mutual regard for expertise and common interests will reap the benefits for the college, local businesses, the community, and especially for students and future employees.

Reference

Wolff, S. J., and Copa, G. H. *New Designs for Career and Technical Education at the Secondary and Postsecondary Levels: Compendium of Design Reviews of Related Research, Policies, and Exemplary Practices*. Minneapolis: University of Minnesota, National Research Center for Career and Technical Education, 2003.

JOHN STUART ERWIN *is president and CEO of Illinois Central College, a state-supported community college in East Peoria, Illinois.*

7

Community colleges often rely on local taxes as an important revenue source and must occasionally seek voter approval for a local mill levy increase—a tax on property to fund a specific activity. This chapter describes strategies for planning and carrying out a campaign for securing that approval.

Sustaining Local Tax Support for Community Colleges: Recommendations for College Leaders

Michael Thomas Miller, Carleton R. Holt

Like public school financing in most states, community college funding has historically been drawn from local taxation. Nationally, about one-fifth of community college revenue is derived from local tax appropriations (State Higher Education Executive Officers, 2004). Although sales tax revenue has traditionally been directed to state general funds, local property taxes are often used to fund K–12 schools and community, junior, and technical colleges (Puyear, 1999). Over half of all states (twenty-nine of them) allow some form of local taxation—including bond issues, property taxation, and sales taxation—for postsecondary education. Many colleges also rely on state-level appropriations, but because the allocation process is somewhat political, and because community colleges often experience reductions in state support during periods of economic difficulty (Kenton, Huba, Schuh, and Shelley, 2005), community colleges in many states continue to rely heavily on local funding to support much of their operating budgets.

One difficulty in relying on state-level funding is the question of equitable distribution: Should state funds be distributed to colleges based on enrollment size, number and types of programs, or the value of property taxes paid to the state government (Martinez and Nodine, 1997)? There is much disagreement about the answer to this question, and the result has been a rise in litigation in nearly half of all states over the equitable distribution and adequacy of funding for public education. Many community colleges are relying on more diverse revenue streams to fund their activities,

NEW DIRECTIONS FOR COMMUNITY COLLEGES, no. 132, Winter 2005 © Wiley Periodicals, Inc.

often looking to contracts with state agencies as a way to replace diminished state general fund allocations and lost local revenue.

In many states, such as Connecticut, the reliance on local taxation for community college resources has led to questions of inequity among public schools, community colleges, and other higher education institutions. In wealthy communities with higher property values, community colleges have been able to generate greater amounts of funding. In other communities, often those with the highest need for postsecondary training and the least access to higher education, low property values and tax revenue do not provide the sums necessary to maintain high-quality community colleges. To balance this inequity, many states have sought to increase state funding for community colleges rather than rely on local property taxes. Currently, only twelve states allow community colleges to fund their operating budgets through property taxes, and thirteen are allowed to fund construction and other major projects by issuing publicly supported bonds with a public vote of approval (King, 1998).

In states where operational funds are derived from local taxes, however, community college leaders must prepare effectively for campaigns to increase and sustain funding, which in some instances includes developing strategies for working with legislators. A *mill levy election* is a process where citizens voluntarily agree to tax their real property to fund a specified activity, such as a school or community college. This strategy is one that community college leaders can employ to sustain local funding for community colleges. To learn more about the process, college leaders can look to the K–12 sector, where mill levy elections are much more common.

The purpose of this chapter is to identify from the research literature five key recommendations for sustaining financial support for community colleges through mill levy elections. The chapter also discusses special considerations for college leaders when addressing or adapting these strategies to local needs and circumstances, concluding with a general discussion of what these strategies mean for community college leaders.

Key Recommendations for Successful Mill Levy Elections

The process of increasing the level of self-taxation for the public good, in this case to fund community college operations, is generally perceived to be open and political. Because community colleges are publicly funded, they cannot openly advocate for an increase in self-taxation—that is, to increase the mill levy—and must do so indirectly through a process of advocacy and collaboration with private coalitions and community groups. To pass a levy increase, college administrators must act outside their official institutional capacity by assuming roles in private citizen groups. Based on practical experience and research-based literature, the following key elements of successful mill levy elections have been identified as recommendations for community college leaders.

Solidify Board Support. Successful millage campaigns start with a vision, and it is the responsibility of the community college president to translate the college's aspirations into goals that can be understood as realistic plans for action. The college's president must facilitate demographic projections, enrollment forecasts, educational assessments, building needs assessments, and resource alternatives. It is imperative that the college's board of trustees or directors unanimously support the idea, and if the president can develop consensus among the board at an early stage, the campaign is more likely to be successful. It may be necessary to make concessions to achieve this support, because a less than unanimous vote by trustees can become fuel for opposition groups in the community.

Board support for a campaign not only bolsters it against opposition groups but also can be an important tool for ensuring the support of highly visible community figures. Several authors have noted that the endorsement of influential community figures has helped school bond election campaigns (Conyers and Francl, 1989; Surratt, 1987; Taylor, 1984), although Crider (1967) found that involvement of political figures, with the exception of city councilors, did not increase the potential for winning such elections. Influential community citizens might be business leaders, the mayor, or civic group leaders. Wheeler (2000) demonstrates the importance of convincing key citizens to become involved in mill levy elections. As he relates, a suburban Chicago superintendent decided her district was in dire need of new facilities. Unfortunately, a previous small referendum had failed miserably only a few years earlier. Therefore, she enlisted the help of the opposition, a group of local citizens called IRATE. The leader of this antitax group had worked actively on behalf of fixed-income senior citizens and had successfully defeated at least $72.5 million in new taxes over the past few years. However, the superintendent convinced him of the district's true need for more money for facility improvement, and he soon became a great supporter and campaigner for the school district, helping the superintendent ask residents to serve on committees to assess school needs. Administrators and school board members were absent from these meetings, so community members were allowed to discover and draw their own conclusions about the millage increase, which they then presented to the school board. The citizen committees eventually took control of the campaign, and the referendum passed.

While formalizing board support for a mill increase or bond campaign, community college administrators should also thoroughly consult state coordinating bodies regarding construction regulations and possible alternative sources of funds. State coordinating bodies can provide a rich reservoir of information, and their resources come at little to no cost and can be critical in planning facility construction or renovation, determining comparable costs, and affirming funding possibilities. Failure to examine these resources thoroughly can provide strength to groups opposed to the proposed mill levy increase.

Use a Citizens' Volunteer Group. Many educators have noted the importance of developing a citizens' volunteer group to gain support in a mill bond campaign. These groups may include faculty and staff members, students, parents, community leaders, some board members (as allowed by law), representative citizens, and administrators. Herman (1991) and Carlson (1990), among many others dating back to the early 1960s (Gott, 1962; Mitchell, 1962), all point to these committees as among the essential elements in successful school bond elections. They also indicate that such committees must be broad-based and represent as many segments of the community as possible. A diverse committee has been found to be a critical defense in dealing with opposition in the community, and such an inclusive practice gives more people a personal stake in the results of the election (Boschee and Holt, 1999).

A community group is used initially to review needs, study alternatives, and make recommendations to go forward. Although it is important to have administrator and staff support for these groups, Holt (1993) found that districts that experienced the greatest success in mill levy elections were those in which administrators played a "low-key" role, allowing members of the supporting volunteer group to assume primary responsibility for educating the public. One of the most important tasks of the citizens' volunteer group is to identify "yes," "no," and "maybe" voters. Research has shown that it is more productive to cultivate the yes and maybe voters, and to spend little time on those who are predisposed to say no. Poll watchers can ensure that all individuals identified as potential yes voters actually make it to the polls. The citizens' volunteer committee should also take the lead in mobilizing the community and raising funds to finance the millage campaign. Legally, community college districts may present factual information to the public, but may not advocate a yes vote. This is the role of the citizens' committee.

Coordinate Community and Media Messages. The process of implementing a campaign to increase tax support should be based on an understanding of what the community sees as important and how the increase in funding will affect its well-being. Romanik (1987) reported that a telephone survey was an effective method of gaining such data, and Graham, Wise, and Backman (1990) advised the use of marketing techniques to determine the target audience and the type of information they needed. Seeing that appropriate information reaches the public has also been identified as critical. Ashe (1959), Mitchell (1962), Crosswait (1967), Nelson (1973), Herman (1991), and Dorweiler and Bittle (1992) all discussed the importance of hiring and using consultants in areas of school planning and finance. In particular, architects and bond consultants can help provide appropriate information to the voting public.

The amount of the millage increase is often based on practicalities, but the public's perception of the amount of the increase is equally as important. According to Holt (1993), the amount of increase in the tax levy requested by a particular district appeared to be a critical element in the success or failure of a bond election. It is also important to address the election from the perspective of the media. College officials should work with the community volunteer group to disseminate important information through print materials such as brochures, flyers, and question and answer sheets. Again, the college should provide factual information to the public, but promotional activities are the responsibility of community volunteer groups. It is imperative, however, to ensure a consistent message in all of the promotional material used in the campaign. This message should underscore the primary reason why the public provides education: student success. When planning for a new or remodeled facility, it is important to remember the impact of a positive climate on student attitudes, emotions, achievement, and learning. College leaders, in conjunction with their community volunteer group, will find that newspapers, radio, and television editors will normally support the needs of education if given a clear explanation of the problems associated with existing facilities and assurances that the millage request is responsible.

Address Technical Considerations. Prior to the announcement of the campaign, college presidents should spend considerable time working with their citizen volunteer committee to formalize and address all of the technical aspects of how the mill levy or bond issue will be conducted. Resources and building plans need to be delineated clearly, and the college president must see that present revenue and spending are clearly accounted for, that maintenance costs of present buildings are explained, that the alternatives to *not* building are believable, that the consequences of not passing the millage are real, that comparative building cost data are presented to the public, and that proposed building sites are the most appropriate. Open, honest dialogue is a prerequisite for success.

The college president and other administrators are primarily responsible for developing the educational specifications of the proposed action, but they should take into account the concerns and ideas of architects, board members, staff, parent representatives, and the business community. Here, the first step is to allow some dreaming to take place. To generate ideas, visit model buildings. College faculty members are also key participants. They should be encouraged to articulate ideal educational environments with the understanding that after a cost analysis, priorities must be selected, and the board will make the final determination. Other technical considerations for community colleges include previous voter turnouts at special elections, the historical success or failure of the college to raise the mill levy or issue bonds, other public agencies' requests of the public, and the economic climate of the college's service area.

Make Use of Successful Election Strategies. Crosswait (1967) and Henry (1987) advocate pursuing a high voter turnout, and suggest that the more educated the voting public, the more likely they will vote in favor of the proposal. The community volunteer committee's activities should include telephone campaigning, door-to-door canvassing, and direct mailings to educate the community about the needs of the college. Personal contacts to share students' needs should be made, employing carefully prepared materials that reflect the range of educational interests served by the college (for example, baccalaureate transfer, retraining programs, basic literacy, and job training). Some successful campaigns have prepared a speaker's notebook for each member of the committee and for those seeking to mobilize yes votes. Another alternative is to prepare a video presentation to ensure a consistent message to all potential voters.

Scholars have reached different conclusions about the effect of the length of the campaign and the date of the election on the ultimate outcome. Crosswait (1967), for example, indicated that the timing of the election date is not a factor in success or failure. Conversely, Mitchell (1962) believed that school bond elections should be held only during the school term, between August and May. Ross (1983) recommended that the campaign start at least one year prior to the election; Conyers and Francl (1989) recommended that referendum campaigning not last longer than thirty days. This means that the process of filing for an election, assembling a citizens' committee, and educating the community should begin well in advance of any expected election. The highly visible, public advocacy of the election, however, should be tightly focused and delivered immediately before the election.

Many studies identify specific problems faced by individual college and school districts. Puzey (1986) and Henry (1987) identified the presence of a strong, organized opposition group as a factor in most failed school bond elections. Gott (1962), and more recently Holt (1993, 2002), identified other factors—most of them out of the college's control—that have a negative effect on election campaigns, such as the size of the school district and the amount of the tax increase. This means that college leaders need to devote a substantial amount of time and energy to understanding the context of the proposed campaign and the environment in which the college operates. In addition to understanding the needs of the college, the president and trustees must understand and be prepared to demonstrate how the welfare of the college directly affects the welfare of the community. In addition, opposition groups and arguments must be identified well in advance if the campaign is to be successful.

Passing a referendum, bond issue, millage, or tax increase of any kind is increasingly difficult because of competition for tax support, competing special interest groups, and an aging population with less interest in public education. College leaders must be prepared to devote a considerable amount of time to understanding the economic and social challenges and opportunities their communities face, and to communicating openly and honestly about their vision for the college. Successful campaigns can provide an impetus for institutions to grow substantially and evolve, but responsibly integrating college services, activities, facilities, and ideology is an important element in allowing this growth to occur.

Implications for College Leaders

Community college leaders have a tremendous responsibility to provide stewardship for public resources and trust. They must effectively communicate with the public, and they must be seen as ethical, trustworthy leaders who have the community's best interests in mind. Sustaining local tax support for community colleges should be seen as a natural extension of this relationship with the community, and must be tied to the overall belief that the college has a responsibility to its local municipality.

One current challenge facing community college presidents is the growing transfer function of their colleges. As community colleges move toward baccalaureate preparation and away from locally focused job training or vocational education, they may have greater difficulty passing mill levy elections because they can be seen as an enabling mechanism for community brain drain. If community colleges want local citizens to fund their operations, they must be aware of how their curriculum affects the community's perception of the institution. This may be particularly true in rural communities where job-training programs are of particular interest and value. In rural communities, community colleges are more than just postsecondary education providers; they serve as focal points for community identification, and they offer cultural enrichment as well as opportunities for leisure and noncredit education.

Leadership training programs for community college presidents need to address ways to sustain local tax support. Attention should be directed toward refining communication skills with the public, understanding the legal limitations on involvement in elections, the role of governing boards in elections, and strategies and techniques for working with community groups. Leadership training programs offered by associations, state bodies, or universities might also review media relations and survey research strategies used in election polling.

The underlying message for community colleges generally—and college leaders specifically—is that they must be purposeful in their actions; their success in community relations is directly correlated to their ability to serve the best interests of the community. Community college leaders must put a significant portion of their time into understanding and diagnosing community needs and relationships, identifying areas in which to expand program offerings, and supporting (and at times challenging) the community's ideals. A college that is positively integrated with its community will have greater success in sustaining financial support, particularly through mill levy elections. The strategies identified in this chapter are important in formalizing the relationships between a college and its community, and can help community colleges fulfill their mission of community service successfully. These same strategies may also be helpful in maintaining a program of legislative support at the state level. Clear communication and a focus on the college's positive contributions to the community's well-being will help college leaders compete for an increasingly limited pool of resources.

References

Ashe, J. L. "An Appraisal of Current Status, Practices, and Procedures in the Use of Fiscal Agents in Relation to School Bond Issues." Unpublished doctoral dissertation, University of Arizona, 1959.

Boschee, F., and Holt, C. R. School Bond Success: A Strategy for Building America's Schools. Lancaster, Pa.: Technomic Publishing, 1999.

Carlson, R. V. "A Rural School/Community: A Dramatic Turnaround and Its Implications for School Improvement." Research in Rural Education, 1990, 7(1), 22–23.

Conyers, J. G., and Francl, T. "We Turned to Madison Avenue for Tips on Selling Our $64 Million Bond Issue." American School Board Journal, 1989, 176(10), 27–28.

Crider, R. J. "Identification of Factors Which Influence the Passage or Failure of School Bond Issues in Selected Counties of Mississippi." Unpublished doctoral dissertation, University of Southern Mississippi, 1967.

Crosswait, B. N. "The Factors Related to the Success and Failure of Bond Issues in the Independent School Districts of South Dakota." Unpublished doctoral dissertation, University of South Dakota, 1967.

Dorweiler, P. J., and Bittle, E. H. "Anatomy of a School Bond Issue." School Business Affairs, 1992, 56(2), 19–23.

Gott, P. L. "Selected Factors Associated with the Success or Failure of School Bond Issue Campaigns in Kentucky." Unpublished doctoral dissertation, Vanderbilt University, 1962.

Graham, G. T., Wise, G. L., and Backman, D. L. Successful Strategies for Marketing School Levies. Fastback no. 310. Bloomington, Ind.: Phi Delta Kappa, 1990.

Henry, J. M. "Help for Passing Bond Referenda." School Business Affairs, 1987, 53(12), 25–27.

Herman, J. J. "Control Points in Planning a New or Remodeled School Building." School Business Affairs, 1991, 57(1), 22–24.

Holt, C. R. "Factors Affecting the Outcomes of School Bond Elections in South Dakota." Unpublished doctoral dissertation, University of South Dakota, 1993.

Holt, C. R. School Bond Success: A Strategy for Building America's Schools (2nd ed.). Lanham, Md.: Scarecrow Press, 2002.

Kenton, C. P., Huba, M. E., Schuh, J. H., and Shelley, M. C. II. "Financing Community Colleges: A Longitudinal Study of 11 States." Community College Journal of Research and Practice, 2005, 29(2) 109–122.

King, D. B. "Successful Community College Selection Strategies." Unpublished doctoral dissertation, University of Arkansas, Fayetteville, 1998.

Martinez, M. C., and Nodine, T. "Michigan: Fiscal Stability and Constitutional Autonomy." In P. Callan and J. E. Finey (eds.), Public and Private Financing of Higher Education. Phoenix: American Council on Education and Oryx Press, 1997.

Mitchell, H. W., Jr. "Identification and Evaluation of Factors Affecting School Bond Issues in Missouri Public Schools." Unpublished doctoral dissertation, University of Missouri, Columbia, 1962.

Nelson, D. C. "An Analysis of Marketing Practices and Net Interest Costs of Selected Bond Issues in Nebraska." Unpublished doctoral dissertation, University of Nebraska, Lincoln, 1973.

Puyear, D. E. Funding Arizona Community Colleges: A Discussion Paper. Phoenix: Arizona State Board of Directors for Community Colleges, 1999.

Puzey, J. "Facing a Hostile Organized Opposition." Paper presented at the annual joint meeting of the Illinois Association of School Boards, Illinois Association of School Administrators, and Illinois Association of School Business Officials, Chicago, Apr. 1986.

Romanik, D. G. *Telephone Survey of Dade County Voters.* Miami, Fla.: Dade County Public Schools, Office of Educational Accountability, 1987.

Ross, V. J. "Don't Be Daunted by Defeat: Score a Bond Issue Victory." *Executive Educator,* 1983, 5(4), 25–26.

State Higher Education Executive Officers. *State Higher Education Finance FY 2004.* Boulder, Colo: State Higher Education Executive Officers, 2004.

Surratt, J. E. "Passing a Bond Issue." Paper presented at the annual meeting of the American Association of School Administrators, New Orleans, Feb. 1987.

Taylor, K. "Bond Elections: Running a Successful Campaign." *ERS Spectrum,* 1984, 2(4), 3–9.

Wheeler, G. "Referendum Gamesmanship." *American School Board Journal,* 2000, 187(1), 46–47.

Michael Thomas Miller is associate professor and coordinator of the program in higher education at the University of Arkansas, Fayetteville.

Carleton R. Holt is assistant professor and graduate coordinator for the program in educational administration at the University of Arkansas, Fayetteville.

8

This chapter describes a proactive, institutionwide budgeting process that is directly tied to a community college district's strategic plan in order to provide community college leaders with the information they need to make judgments about cutting or sustaining programs in difficult economic times.

Using Strategic Planning to Transform a Budgeting Process

Cary A. Israel, Brenda Kihl

Today's community college leaders face a challenging financial climate not seen in several decades. Budget shortfalls, state budget cuts, high unemployment, increased health care costs, and decreased tax revenue create challenging economic times for community colleges and require difficult decision making to maintain a strong, financially sound institution that succeeds in serving its constituents. The questions college leaders face are familiar: Where can we cut spending? Which programs need paring back and how far? How and where can we reduce fixed costs? How can we increase revenue streams? Do we need to make reductions in our labor force? Where do we invest new revenue? These questions are difficult to address without incurring potential negative effects on students, staff, faculty, and the community. However, the negative impacts can be minimized by making clear and logical decisions that are supported by the institution's strategic budgeting and planning processes. This chapter describes how the Collin County Community College District (Texas) answered these difficult questions, and discusses steps taken to control spending, make the most of limited resources, and incorporate the district's strategic plan into the budgeting process.

Addressing Rapidly Changing Economic Conditions

Collin County Community College District (CCCCD) is a five-campus district in a historically affluent county in North Texas. Enrolling more than forty thousand credit and noncredit students annually, the district serves suburban and rural communities covering nearly one thousand square

NEW DIRECTIONS FOR COMMUNITY COLLEGES, no. 132, Winter 2005 © Wiley Periodicals, Inc.

miles, with a population of approximately seven hundred thousand. CCCCD opened its doors amid the strong economic climate of 1985. Located in Texas's "Telecom Corridor," CCCCD flourished during the technology boom of the late 1990s. During that decade, Collin County's population grew by 150 percent, and CCCCD's enrollment rose by 57 percent. Prior to 2001, the district had never known difficult economic times, and never had to consider difficult budgetary decisions. This changed in the fall of 2001, when downturns in the telecommunications and airline industries, the area's two economic bellwethers, began to require mass layoffs.

Before 2001 CCCCD received the majority of its revenue from local property taxes (44 percent), and significant amounts from state appropriations (28 percent), tuition and fees (15 percent), and other sources, such as grants and auxiliary services (13 percent). Tuition income remained low because the district's board of trustees has always been committed to affordable education and opposes significant tuition increases. Unfortunately, this left the institution extremely vulnerable to economic downturns and dependent on increases in property values and state appropriations. In 2000, CCCCD was not in a financial position to withstand a significant decrease in state or local revenue, yet this was about to occur.

State funding for Texas community colleges is calculated using an instructional formula based on contact hour reimbursement. Each biennium, the Texas legislature sets a rate to which it will reimburse colleges for instructional costs incurred. Between 1994 and February 2003, Texas's contributions to the community college instructional formula fell from 86.9 percent to 51.8 percent (Texas Association of Community Colleges, 2003). Local property taxes could not make up the difference in revenue. The district was already collecting local taxes at its maximum rate of nine cents per hundred dollars of assessed value, one of the lowest rates in Texas. With a depressed economy, it was unlikely that county voters would approve an increase in the property tax rate to support the community college. These circumstances made it increasingly evident that district leaders must make significant changes to their operating procedures to ensure long-term financial stability.

The Coming Economic Storm and Enhanced Environmental Scanning

In 2000, CCCCD's leaders determined that a more comprehensive environmental scanning process would help prepare for the future and improve the district's ability to withstand changes in the economy. All community college leaders analyze enrollment trends, such as the market share of high school graduates attending our institutions; growth and decline of specific disciplines; the overall general economic climate of our communities; faculty salary requirements, retirements, and new hires; and other factors that affect the budgeting and planning processes. As members of CCCCD's leadership team, we monitored this information closely. However, like many institutions, we did not track other factors that might be better indicators of the overall economic vitality of our service areas.

Anticipating drastic changes in the economy, CCCCD instituted an environmental scanning process in 2000 that monitors and tracks these other factors, detailed here, to help us predict where the economy was going and to develop a realistic three-year budget plan. This scanning also made us aware of pending challenges and allowed us to develop what-if scenarios as economic conditions changed (as they indeed did). We thus started to track the volume of food stamps awarded in Collin County over a five-year period, to see if we could identify trends that could help predict the economic future of our community. We also tracked trends in Temporary Assistance for Needy Families, sales tax allocations, and residential building permits. In addition, we monitored home foreclosures, local public school lunch program recipients, indigent health care claims, small business bankruptcies, the state's rainy day fund, appraised property tax growth rate, and companies moving in and out of Collin County. Nearly all of this information was readily available from the county, regional council of governments, the state comptroller, the Small Business Administration, the realtors' association, financial institutions, and the district's small business development center.

Our environmental scanning paid off. Residents in Collin County were hit hard by the 2001 downturn in the economy, which also had a significant budgetary impact on the district. Unemployment rates reported by the Texas Workforce Commission (2005) showed a 163 percent increase from October 2000 to October 2001, and this had a precipitous effect on other economic factors in Collin County and throughout Texas. Newspapers reported other disturbing trends; the Collin County home foreclosure rate for the month of January increased over 300 percent between 2001 and 2004 (Graham, 2003). In addition, indigent health care claims were climbing steadily, and requests for free lunch programs at our local school districts were soaring. Indeed, the percentage of economically disadvantaged students was growing rapidly; in 1999, the district disbursed $2.5 million in financial aid, scholarships, and federal and state grants. By 2000 that number doubled to nearly $5 million, and in 2004 the district disbursed more than $12 million in financial aid. Moreover, local businesses were moving out, closing, or going bankrupt faster than those that were relocating or being created. Texas's rainy day fund was moving toward deficit, and interest rates were beginning to drop.

Despite these disturbing trends, our community was still seeing record population growth. Had we just concentrated on population growth and housing starts—traditional measures used in planning for enrollment growth—we might have concluded that the economy was still fiscally sound. Yet by scanning a more expansive set of environmental data, we knew that it was a matter of time before funding for the district and other community colleges in the state would be cut.

At the fall 2000 State of the District presentation, the president discussed these alarming statistics. Although some individuals disagreed that the economy might be on the verge of a downturn, most began to discuss the findings. Against this backdrop, we started to plan for the district's future so that we could minimize the impact of any revenue loss. After thoughtfully discussing and planning a course of action, we decided to develop a very conservative budget that anticipated the coming economic meltdown. Although the practice of environmental scanning may not always be an accurate economic gauge, we believe it helped our college move to a more strategic budgeting process. We continue to employ all the external environmental data at our disposal in order to plan for a fast-changing economic landscape.

Planning for Shrinking Resources

Environmental scanning data led us to believe an economic storm was coming, so we began to plan for shrinking resources. The first order of business was stabilizing and reducing expenditures.

Reducing Instructional Costs. To reduce expenditures, we first looked at the cost of instruction, because it makes up the largest proportion of the overall budget. It was imperative that any budget cuts in this area not inhibit the district's ability to accommodate its growing student population and maintain academic excellence. However, we were able to reduce the number of extra faculty stipends and contracts by limiting them to only those services essential to the quality of our educational offerings. For example, we cut instructional release time for faculty serving as treasurers of faculty constituency groups, because the duties of the office required far less time than teaching a semester-long course. In addition, we challenged college deans to increase the average class size from nineteen students per section to twenty-three rather than adding new sections to accommodate enrollment growth. The deans had flexibility to run some classes with fewer students but were strongly encouraged to keep the average divisional class size at twenty-three. These initial steps reduced spending without adversely affecting instructional quality or student services.

Analyzing Third-Party Expenditures. In addition, we started examining existing partnerships with third parties (such as foodservice agencies, those who rent our facilities, and local agencies that are freely allowed to use campus facilities) to ensure that equitable relationships existed. Historically, although the district did not charge rent to local economic development agencies for their use of college office space, the cities charged the district to rent their facilities for graduation and commencement ceremonies, as well as other functions. By correcting this imbalance, CCCD saved thousands of dollars. This was but one of many examples of the ways in which we saved money by thoroughly analyzing third-party expenditures. It was not easy to renegotiate these informal arrangements, but an increased focus on external communications allowed city and county leaders to understand our budget predicament. Indeed, through this experience we learned that there are always opportunities to be more fiscally conservative without jeopardizing instruction or professional development.

Replacing Revenue Bonds with General Obligation Bonds. Texas state law requires local community college districts—not the state—to fund construction of new facilities. To accommodate enrollment growth in the early 1990s, a bond referendum was proposed to fund new buildings and deferred maintenance but was defeated by area voters. Because new classrooms had to be built to accommodate enrollment growth, CCCCD's board of trustees issued revenue bonds to accomplish this goal. But the revenue bonds carried higher interest rates and were a drag on our operating funds. We knew that this issue needed to be remedied before revenue streams, particularly those from state sources, eroded. Thus, in early 2001, the district decided to ask voters to pass a $57 million general obligation bond. The timing of this initiative was both crucial and fortuitous. The economic bubble had not yet burst, and enrollment was mushrooming. Fortunately, voters overwhelmingly passed the bond referendum, which significantly relieved pressures on our operating budget. Our strategic budget preparation and forecasting processes made us realize the interconnectivity of disparate budget lines.

Making Miscellaneous Budget Cuts. Although CCCCD was able to shrink its budget by cutting extra instructional costs, reducing third-party expenditures, and moving toward lower-interest bonds, much more had to be accomplished to align the district's budget with anticipated revenue cuts. We consolidated administrative functions, revamped an uncapped salary grid, closed poorly enrolled programs, created a continuing education profit center, discontinued leisure classes, bought down the debt of callable high-interest revenue bonds, and established a three-year salary schedule for faculty and staff. All in all, though some decisions were difficult and challenging, our planning paid off. When the economic storm hit, our academic classes remained open and accessible, agreed-upon salary increases were honored, more students were admitted, and new academic programs were created.

With spending brought under control, we also began looking at other sources of revenue to supplement existing streams. We established CCCCD's first deferred giving program, set lofty fundraising goals, increased federal and state grant awards tied to our strategic plan, and planned other revenue-generating activities. Concurrent with these activities, we began to revamp a traditional incremental budget process and move toward one that is more strategic and responsive to changing economic conditions.

From Incremental to Strategic Budgeting

In 2000, an internal survey of CCCCD's budget process and financial management revealed the need for change, and college leaders began planning to strengthen their budgeting and planning processes. At that time, the district's budget process consisted of annual incremental increases based on the overall amount of revenue. Each division received the same percentage increase over the prior year's allocation and was not required to submit evidence of need or prove effective use of funds. Budget managers maintained the status quo and were not challenged to move strategically beyond established processes (Ibrahim and Proctor, 1992). The incremental budgeting system in place in 2000 could not prepare the district for the coming downturn in the local economy.

The district's practice of incremental budgeting provided too much latitude, and it did not hold managers accountable for their budgeting decisions. The process also created administrative "silos" within CCCCD, rather than creating a sense of interdependence and team. CCCCD's incremental budgeting process also committed funds to certain budget areas without evidence that the base allocation or additional monies were needed to meet and accomplish institutional goals. The incremental process assumed that the district's priorities remained constant, which prevented leaders from launching new initiatives or providing access to additional resources to support growing areas of the district (Curry, 2000). Furthermore, several top-level administrators did not have a working knowledge of their budgets and found it acceptable to delegate fiscal responsibilities to administrative assistants. This proved to be a significant barrier to making difficult choices about funding priorities as the economy changed. In this age of data-driven decision making, budget managers must be accountable for their finances and make decisions in support of the institution's strategic plan. Thus, it soon became evident that the first step in building a financially sound institution was to modify the budgeting system and make budget managers accountable. CCCCD also realized that departments and programs change over time, and that base allocations should be flexible too. A new budgeting system was needed to distribute funds based on something other than "steady state" existence.

Accordingly, we decided to conduct a series of administrative meetings in spring 2000 to discuss budget responsibility and the goals of the coming years. The district president informed vice presidents and deans that the current culture must change and they would no longer be rewarded for overbudgeting (hoarding money) or allowed to continue the practice of underbudgeting. In these meetings it became evident that administrators must thoroughly understand and effectively plan their budgets. The district's three-year strategic planning process became the launching point for setting funding priorities and addressing the difficult funding decisions that lay ahead.

Zero-Sum Budgeting

Effective budgeting systems for community colleges must possess the stabilizing processes found in an incremental budgeting system to minimize annual justification of obvious institutional necessities. However, the process must also incorporate a *zero-based* budgeting system that allows for questioning and minimizing redundant expenses (Williams, 1981). The destabilizing process of zero-based budgeting, unfortunately, requires all expenditures to be justified each new period, which is a time-consuming process (Curry, 2000). Neither of these common budgeting practices alone fits the district's vision and changing needs. College leaders had to establish a new model that would meet the four purposes of an effective budget: continuity, change, flexibility, and rigidity (Wildavsky, 1978).

Thus CCCCD decided to move to a form of *zero-sum* budgeting, a deficit-neutral budget process, where new expenditures are paid through cuts in existing programs or increases in revenue. Keeping the district's mission and strategic plan in mind, leaders adopted a modified zero-sum process to help make decisions that could reduce unnecessary or wasteful spending, streamline and minimize costs, and strengthen revenue streams. Our desired result was a static bottom line, with no direct annual increases in expenditures. In order to accommodate the needs of growing programs, new initiatives, and achievement indicators outlined in the strategic plan, we added a supplemental budget request process.

The Budget Process. A zero-sum budgeting process takes about four months and begins with an allocation for each of a college president's direct reports (for example, vice presidents and provosts). These allocations are equal to the previous year's budget, minus a formula reduction for line items that had spent less than 50 percent of allocations at midyear. Vice presidents and provosts then distribute this lump allocation among their respective division managers. Each division manager, who may be a dean, director, or coordinator, is responsible for the budget of one or more departments. At this point in the budget process, division managers have the flexibility to reallocate resources between budget lines and across departmental budgets in their division. In the end, division managers propose a budget that is less than or equal to the previous year's budget. However, supplemental budget requests allow for increased allocations for costs associated with CCCCD's three-year strategic plan (Collin County Community College District, 2004).

Each vice president and provost then compiles preliminary budgets and associated supplemental requests from division managers, and if necessary, further reallocates resources; for example, underspending in one division can meet the supplemental requests in another. Vice presidents, provosts, and their division managers negotiate budgets and justifications for supplemental requests. The communication and information-sharing that occurs during this negotiation phase ensures that managers are more accommodating of other divisions' needs (Taylor and Rafai, 2003). Ultimately, it is the vice presidents' or provosts' responsibility to ensure an overall adherence to the initial allocation and the district's strategic plan. A budget must be agreed upon in order to move to the next step in the budgeting process, where each budget is examined in open hearings.

Open Hearings. Open budget hearings take place over the course of a week. One at a time, the president, vice presidents, provosts, and division managers defend their budgets to CCCCD's leadership team, finance department, and each other. Hearings require division managers to answer questions and explain significant changes—both positive and negative—in any one budget or individual line item. Supplemental requests are also reviewed during the hearings to ensure that additional funds will meet the goals and achievement indicators outlined in the district's strategic plan. Open hearings are time-consuming, but the public venue requires all employees with fiscal responsibilities to have a rationale for the amount allocated to each line item in their budget.

The budget hearings also serve to provide budget managers, college leaders, and other responsible budget personnel with a broader, "beyond-the-silo" perspective of college operations. Through the process, budget managers realize there is no "hidden" money in district budgets, and they can no longer hoard excess money that will not be used. They also learn about the importance of deferred maintenance costs, bond interest payments, fund balances, encumbered payroll lines, and all the other categories that affect the district's overall budget. On conclusion of the budget hearings, the leadership team considers organizational priorities and makes a finalized budget proposal to CCCCD's board of trustees.

Drawbacks and Benefits of Zero-Sum Budgeting. A disadvantage of zero-sum budgeting is the potential for competition between managers, because money is reallocated from one department to another. However, implementing a process for requesting supplemental funds alleviates the competitive element of zero-sum budgeting and helps mitigate begging for new funds. At the same time, it forces the leadership team to identify and eliminate funding for lower priorities in order to fund new initiatives. Budget managers also understand that extra funds can come at the expense of an existing program if projected revenue falls short of the overall budget increase, and this knowledge helps create internal accountability. Over time, training for midlevel budget managers, combined with a budgeting hearing process that ties internal budgeting processes directly to the district's strategic plan, significantly broadened CCCCD leaders' understanding of how to manage scarce resources prudently.

Where Are We Now?

As this chapter is being written in summer 2005, we are confident that CCCCD is spending its money better and that because of changes in our budgeting process expenditures are more aligned to our strategic plan. By implementing a more comprehensive environmental scanning process to predict the economic environment, and by moving from incremental to strategic budgeting, we were able to make difficult decisions more easily. We are not yet out of the woods, however. Community college leaders will always be required to make difficult decisions, but they can do so with forethought and planning to minimize negative impact and public opposition.

In 2003, our strategic planning process was put to the test. Texas faced a record deficit of $9.9 billion (Hill, 2004), and legislators were challenged to balance the budget. All public colleges and universities were mandated to cut their state appropriation by 7.5 percent, which resulted in a $1.5 million reduction in the district's operating budget. Because of foresight and careful planning, however, the overall impact of this budget cut was minimized. The district's finances were already under control, a new budgeting system was in place, and new revenue sources slightly decreased our dependence on local taxes and state appropriations. The difficult decisions CCCCD made in 2000 and 2001 paid off, making the district financially and administratively stronger.

Keys to Creating a Strategic Budgeting Process

Planning and accountability are keys to weathering economic downturns and sustaining funding for community colleges. It is imperative that academic, student development, and technology plans be aligned with a college's overall financial plan. This is undoubtedly a major undertaking, but it is a necessary step in achieving financial stability. This plan must then be communicated to all who are involved with or who have a vested interest in the community college.

Budget cuts are rarely met with excitement. Therefore, effective communication with college stakeholders, including faculty, staff, students, the board of trustees, and the community at large, is vitally important to continued success. Key stakeholders must buy in to any strategic budget in order to minimize opposition to any necessary future budget cuts. At CCCCD, internal stakeholder communication takes place at the annual All College Day, which all faculty and staff are required to attend. The president delivers a State of the District address to ensure that all college employees understand the current economic climate and its impact on college operations. In addition, the district has established the "Committee of 100"—a group of community and business leaders—to facilitate external communication. The committee comes together every three years, is educated on the state of CCCCD, and brainstorms the strategic direction the district should follow over the next three years. Such community involvement not only helps disseminate information about a college's needs and goals to the general population but also allows a more informed public to better understand the difficult decisions community college leaders face.

Our advice for community college leaders facing tough economic times is to focus on your college's mission, goals, and strategic plan, the fundamental elements that describe your institution and its future. Internal planning and budgeting processes must support these fundamental elements if your college is to survive when funds are limited. Institutional constituents must accept the college's mission, goals, and strategic plan if they are to support the tough decisions that must be made in a challenging economic climate. For this reason, it is essential to develop a comprehensive training program for senior staff and midlevel budget managers and ensure high levels of communication when difficult decisions are necessary. CCCCD's move from incremental to strategic budgeting clearly helped us withstand a downturn in the Texas economy and diminished state revenues, and we believe it can help other institutions as well.

References

Collin County Community College District. "Strategic Goals and Achievement Indicators 2004–2006." Plano, Tex.: Collin County Community College District, 2004.

Curry, J. R. "Budgeting." In C. M. Grills (ed.), *College and University Business Administration* (6th ed.). Washington, D.C.: National Association of College and University Business Officers, 2000.

Graham, L. "Home Foreclosures Soar Amid Jobless Recovery." *Frisco Enterprise,* Dec. 26, 2003, n.p. http://www.zwire.com/site/news.cfm?newsid=10717727&BRD=1426&PAG=461&dept_id=528197&rfi=6. Accessed May 16, 2005.

Hill, I. "State Responses to Budget Crises in 2004: Texas." Washington, D.C.: The Urban Institute, 2004. http://www.urban.org/UploadedPDF/410955_TX_budget_crisis.pdf#search='texas%20state%20budget%20deficit%2020042004. Accessed May 17, 2005.

Ibrahim, M. M., and Proctor, R. A. "Incremental Budgeting in Local Authorities." *International Journal of Public Sector Management,* 1992, 5(5), 11–26.

Taylor, A., and Rafai, S. "Strategic Budgeting: A Case Study and Proposal Framework." *Management Accounting Quarterly,* 2003, 5(1), 1–10.

Texas Association of Community Colleges. "Community College Formula Appropriation FY 1990–91 to FY 2004–05." Austin: Texas Association of Community Colleges, 2003. http://www.tacc.org/pdf/ctc_formula_tacc.pdf. Accessed May 19, 2005.

Texas Workforce Commission. "Unemployment (LAUS)." Austin: Texas Workforce Commission, 2005. http://www.tracer2.com/cgi/dataanalysis/AreaSelection.asp?tableName=Labforce. Accessed May 4, 2005.

Wildavsky, A. "A Budget for All Seasons? Why the Traditional Budget Lasts." *Public Administration Review,* 1978, 38(6), 501–509.

Williams, J. J. "Designing a Budgeting System with Planned Confusion." *California Management Review,* 1981, 24(2), 75–85.

CARY A. ISRAEL *is president of Collin County Community College District.*

BRENDA KIHL *is assistant to the president and director of the Center for Teaching, Learning, and Professional Development at Collin County Community College District.*

9

This chapter examines challenges and options available to community college presidents as their institutions increasingly rely on unstable revenue streams. Presidents, particularly those at institutions with limited access to strong local tax support, require new and expanded fiscal leadership skills.

The Changing Role of the President as a Fiscal Leader

Daniel J. Phelan

Presidents, chancellors, and other campus leaders face what seems like an ever-increasing number of fiscal pressures as they seek to meet the expanding needs of their constituency while balancing a stressed budget. Financial management has always constituted an important part of the president's role, but both the percentage of the leaders' time given to this function and its intensity have changed remarkably in recent years. Continuing financial difficulties, particularly at the state level, require community college presidents to develop and cultivate a new set of skills.

In 2002, the American Council on Education issued the fifth in a series of reports on the American college president. The 2,594 college and university presidents surveyed for this study were instructed to indicate the four activities in which they spend the most time (thus, the following percentages exceed 100 percent). Highest-ranked functions were, in order of significance, planning (59.3 percent), fundraising (56.6 percent), and budgeting (50.5 percent). However, when the data were controlled for institutional type, public two-year presidents listed their primary tasks (also in order of significance) as planning (56.2 percent), community relations (56.2 percent), and personnel management (54.6 percent). Community college presidents spent about 47.8 percent of their time budgeting and 32 percent in fundraising efforts, suggesting that time spent on the finance function has not exceeded other traditional aspects of college operations.

Mark Milliron, former CEO of the League for Innovation in the Community College, suggested that now is the time to redirect the president's focus: "It's a different time in the community college world. And that

NEW DIRECTIONS FOR COMMUNITY COLLEGES, no. 132, Winter 2005   © Wiley Periodicals, Inc.

means that we need to think about the new skill sets that presidents will need" (Evelyn, 2004, p. A28). Evelyn (2004) suggested that those skills included the ability to obtain private donations, grants, and federal support.

Given the ever-changing social dynamic associated with institutional direction and financial health, essential skill sets for all presidents must expand beyond those of simply lobbying for legislative support, raising tuition and fees, and pursuing additional local tax dollars. Community college leaders must demonstrate acuity in following legislative and congressional activities and must become personally involved in the process. They should also develop skills in assessing and pursuing capital and planned gifts, critically evaluating institutional core competencies and functions central to the college's mission, advancing efforts leading to the creation and alignment of partnerships and corporate alliances, selling nonessential assets and services, managing human resources, acquiring technologies that advance the organization, closely managing insurance and health care costs, outsourcing, generating profit through auxiliary services, improving debt management strategies, and above all, fostering an entrepreneurial spirit across the college. After briefly discussing the need for community college leaders to hone new financial skills, this chapter discusses the two-year college's main revenue streams, as well as the president's role in maximizing revenue and financial stability.

The Need for Change

According to McClenney (2004), increasing fiscal pressures come at a time when the demand for employees with a postsecondary degree is nearing its peak, and as baby boomers begin to retire. Quite possibly, impending retirements will create a gap between a burgeoning need for workers and a college's ability to respond with trained students. This gap will occur, in part, as the result of reduced local, state, and federal support for community colleges. In some cases, reduced funding has resulted in the stagnation, reduction, or even elimination of instructional programs and services, as well as reduced student access to a community college education.

The National Center for Public Policy and Higher Education (2004) reports that increases in tuition and declining state appropriations have resulted in reduced access to postsecondary education for over 250,000 students across the country. In Michigan, state aid for community colleges was reduced by over 15 percent between 2001 and 2005, and projections suggest additional cuts in 2006. Furthermore, throughout the federal budget development process, the Bush administration has proposed program eliminations, reductions, and only modest increases for a number of higher education programs. Interestingly, President Bush's proposal for a $100 increase in the Pell grant program was followed by New York Governor Pataki's announcement of a $500 increase in tuition. These funding reductions and less-than-inflation-rate adjustments, combined with tuition increases, not only limit access to needy students but concomitantly increase the financial aid burden on states and institutions. The rapid decline in state funding gives community college leaders little choice but to accept a changed fiscal landscape for their colleges. It challenges them to master the new and expanding skills necessary to keep colleges fiscally viable, as well as to ensure access to the very people who need the community college most.

Declining State Support: The President as Lobbyist

As state support for community colleges has declined, the general relationship between states and institutions of higher education has changed; colleges receive less money, and are forced to compete with health care and K–12 institutions for limited state funds. These changes create a dilemma for two-year college leaders. One college president described the conflicted situation of serving more students with reduced state support this way: "We have a moral responsibility to grow to educate more students, and a fiscal responsibility not to do so unless funding patterns change" (American Council on Education, 2004, p. 3).

Certainly, one can argue that the receding fiscal tide of state support for community colleges is synchronous with the ups and downs of the national economy. In the past, community college presidents may have spun a bad fiscal situation by saying, "We just need to hang on a bit longer and things will eventually improve." However, many states report that— even in a positive national economy—state support for community college operating budgets still wanes. As long as community colleges are funded through states' discretionary budgets, and as long as there is increased competition for these funds, college fiscal leaders should expect instability in state funding streams. Consequently, today's community college presidents should be skilled in building significant relationships with legislators. Where possible, college presidents should leverage legislators' constituents, including college trustees, students, retirees, and local business leaders, to make the case for strong state support. The president should also have at command a "telephone tree" of selected community members to be called on at a moment's notice to write letters, make telephone calls, and send e-mails to legislators about vital funding legislation. To be sure, this practice will require significant time and effort to orchestrate, but this is the price of admission to the legislative table.

Because most community colleges cannot afford to hire a lobbyist, the president becomes the de facto lobbyist. It is imperative for the college leader to develop skills in this area. As the American Council on Education (2002) noted, "The increasing use of student aid, while state funding declines as a proportion of revenue, will make all institutions of higher education more sensitive to market pressures. These trends and others may require that new presidents come prepared with extensive skills in academic leadership, financial management, and political negotiation honed by diverse career experiences" (p. 48). Community college presidents can obtain and hone these political skills through formal training, through counsel from former legislators and lobbyists, or through workshops conducted by a variety of national organizations.

Presidents should also work with their local governing board or foundation board to establish special funding for a "placeholder account." These funds, included as part of the president's total compensation package and subject to taxation, should be used to support both candidates running for office and those currently in office. Make no mistake, campaign contributions provide access to important policymakers; community colleges cannot afford to be on the outside looking in when legislation and state funding are being debated.

Tuition and Fees: The President as Defender

Raising tuition and fees has always been one of the few tools available to community college presidents and boards of trustees as they try to balance revenues against the costs of operation. However, without responsible fiscal stewardship, even this avenue for improved funding is at risk. More specifically, as a result of tuition increases that regularly exceed cost-of-living and consumer price indexes and that have been made with unclear or unconvincing rationales, public and state legislatures are scrutinizing community colleges more closely. Concern over rising tuition has resulted in attempts to implement price controls and threats of federal penalties. For example, congressional representatives from Ohio and California have repeatedly decried the significant rise in charges to students. In their congressional analysis of higher education costs Boehner and McKeon (2003) stated: "The ongoing cost explosion is a disturbing trend, and one that cannot be allowed to continue" (p. 1). In addition, both representatives expressed concern that tuitions have been raised following increases in federal financial aid, and together have repeatedly introduced legislation that ties tuition increases to consumer price indexes. They have also tried to implement harsh consequences for institutions of higher education that repeatedly exceed those limits.

Similar constraints have also surfaced in individual states. For example, Governor Jennifer Granholm (2005) of Michigan, with support in the state legislature, signed into law a bill that promised to give community colleges a 3 percent rebate (from a 15 percent reduction in state aid that had occurred over the previous four years) if institutions kept their tuition and fee increases below the Detroit consumer price index of 1.9 percent. In addition, the governor promised no additional cuts in state aid support for 2005. Those colleges choosing to ignore the proposal would not receive the 3 percent rebate, not have protection against cuts in 2005, and would be required to pay 3 percent of their current support back to the state. Needless to say, all of the state's twenty-eight community colleges opted to take the governor's deal.

Unfortunately, about seven months later, and even though the community colleges did not raise their tuition or fees more than 1.9 percent, Governor Granholm implemented a $4.9 million cut in aid to community colleges in order to settle the state's 2005 budget shortfall (Bernthal, 2005). To be fair, some of the institutions received other fiscal resources (such as restricted-use maintenance and capital outlay funding) as part of the proposal, yet these were not in keeping with the original agreement. This is an example of what can happen in a state as a result of dramatic budget problems and changing fiscal priorities. Community college leaders must be prepared to address these sometimes glaring inconsistencies through regular scenario planning and by developing budget contingencies.

Community college presidents must also hone other skills in the area of tuition and fees, including developing strong relationships with students, parents, and the media in order to communicate the need for tuition and fee increases. Public skepticism of tuition and fee increases requires that intuitional leaders and their governing boards ensure the effectiveness of all expenditures. Furthermore, the president and the governing board must clearly articulate their reasons for increasing tuition if they are going to maintain the confidence of their constituency. As Boswell (2004) stated, "Community college leaders have a responsibility to reexamine their own practices and assumptions, holding themselves accountable for adopting cost-effective and learning-centered strategies that help ensure student success" (p. 49). Long gone are the days of simply raising tuition rates without critical fiscal introspection and valid justification. Failure to undertake this assessment will invariably (and perhaps deservedly) invoke public comment and criticism.

Local Support: The President as Spokesperson and Marketing Choreographer

As Chapter One notes, local support was a major—if not the single most important—funding source for early junior colleges in this country, largely because they were extensions of local school systems. Today, however, community colleges can obtain revenues from property taxes in their political or school district boundaries in only twenty-six states. In some cases, the college may have statutory authority to levy a tax for specific needs (for example, facility improvement or debt retirement). In other cases, the college may be dependent on support from a majority of registered voters in order to obtain additional funding for defined college needs. Sources of local support vary highly between states, and in some cases, within states.

Increasingly (and unfortunately), it appears that a community college education is perceived by local residents as more of a "private good" than a "public good," thereby limiting the public's desire to support two-year institutions (American Council on Education, 2004; Boswell, 2004). There are some exceptions to this sentiment. Most notably, in November 2004 Arizona voters approved (by a 76 percent margin) over $951 million in general obligation bonds so that the Maricopa Community College District could build new classrooms and improve facilities, energy efficiency, instructional technology, and land acquisitions. Similarly, voters in the Dallas County Community College District approved a $450 million bond referendum with more than a 70 percent margin in May 2004.

Other colleges, however, particularly rural institutions with lower assessed property valuations and colleges in areas with flat or declining population bases, struggle to obtain additional local support to make up for the declining state investment (Katsinas, Palmer, and Tollefson, 2004). Jackson Community College (Michigan), for example, has been unable to convince voters of the need for additional property tax revenues. The college's only local tax support was obtained in 1964, and is in regression because of a legislatively mandated inflationary adjustment, resulting in a declining tax rate. The institution has unsuccessfully placed an increase in property taxes on the ballot on eleven separate occasions, at different points during the calendar year, for varying purposes, and for different lengths of time. Focus group interviews about ballot questions in 2003 and 2004 revealed a belief among voters that students should pay more because they are the direct recipients of postsecondary education. In one instance, participants suggested that students should pay upwards of $125 to $150 per credit hour before the college should seek taxpayer assistance. Sadly, voters had little understanding of the econometric benefits that accrue as a result of an educated populace, even though the college had conducted and reported the results of a major economic study showing just that.

To deal with issues of local tax support, community college presidents must strengthen their relationship- and partnership-building skills with the public, media, local government, regional employers, local school districts, and other taxing entities. The president and the board must be able to clearly and repeatedly articulate the institution's value to the broader community. As the American Council on Education (2002) noted, "Questions continue to swirl around the issues of college costs and quality. Institutional leaders must be prepared to deliver the message of higher education's pivotal role in economic growth, research, and technological advancement" (p. 48).

The president and governing board should also be engaged in intergovernmental discussions about the college's future direction, the needs of the community and the region, and the need for additional support. College leaders must build, and in this age of ballot recall elections, sustain a coalition of support if they are to have any chance of obtaining a millage, bond, or tax levy. Once consensus builds for additional assistance, community college leaders must clearly define and establish community college funding as a priority among various other community needs.

Furthermore, it is essential for community college leaders to have strong relationships with local school superintendents so they can stage the timing of tax support requests. Taxpayers often react poorly when faced with multiple and competing requests for their help. Thus, if either entity is to be successful at the polls, K–12 and community college leaders must work collaboratively. In most cases, this will require a high degree of trust among institutions, long-range planning, and patience for a turn at the ballot box. Governing board involvement in these relationships must be sustained over time.

Finally, community college presidents must give significant attention to the care and feeding of the community. Presidents are the primary spokespeople and marketing choreographers for their colleges. As such, they must ensure that the public is ever-aware of their existence, mission, outcomes, and benefit to the region. For example, the president should provide for the timely, regular, and strategic distribution of information about college activities, faculty and staff involvement in the community, human interest features about students and employees, accreditation renewal, significant board initiatives, economic development impact, instructional quality, and awards received.

To be sure, building relationships with the community takes considerable time and must be attended to constantly. Like Covey's reference (1992) to the law of the harvest, one cannot expect to ignore the nurturing and cultivation of this relationship for long periods of time and then expect to receive a bountiful harvest of funding in short order. Relationship-building with college constituents must be a continuous and thoughtful activity. Failing to keep the college in the forefront of the community's social consciousness—particularly in today's fifteen-second sound bite and media-overloaded world—is to put the college at risk of declines in local tax support.

Federal Support: The President as Advocate

Federal support for community colleges comes in two basic forms, indirect and direct. Indirect support includes student financial aid, by far the federal government's largest investment in community colleges. Direct federal support for community colleges includes workforce training and other grant-funded activities, such as the Carl D. Perkins Vocational and Technical Education Act, which supports postsecondary vocational and technical education programs, as well as Workforce Investment and Tech Prep, which are often administered by state agencies. Other federal grant sources include Title III, the National Science Foundation, and the Fund for the Improvement of Postsecondary Education, all of which are obtained on a competitive basis.

Unfortunately, less than 3 percent of the total federal budget is allocated to education; direct federal aid to community colleges represents only a small percentage of an institution's budget. Federal funding for community colleges may plummet further with the help of some members in Congress who plan to introduce a "single definition" of a postsecondary institution into the reauthorization of the Higher Education Act; this would provide proprietary, for-profit colleges with access to direct federal aid (Boehner and McKeon, 2004). The consequence of this change, if it occurs, will be to severely limit the amount of funds that go to public institutions of higher education. It is sometimes difficult to understand why some in Congress would want to augment for-profit institutions' operating revenues, because they have shareholders, pay dividends, and charge high tuition to students.

Clearly, over the past several years, there has been a significant departure from the ways community colleges were traditionally funded. Declining federal support, both in real dollars and as a percentage of institutional operating budgets, continues to challenge the comprehensive mission of the community college. Still, community college leaders must be involved with their local workforce investment boards in order to access dollars to promote job training and economic development. Furthermore, presidents must be fluent with student aid policies and Higher Education Act funding provisions, and should be vigilant with regard to new and proposed changes in federal laws. Presidents and their governing boards should actively and regularly contact their elected officials in Washington and make their positions known. College leaders should also team up with their colleagues across the country, as well as with the American Association of Community Colleges and the Association of Community College Trustees, to coordinate the message to congressional staffers and members of Congress. Like it or not, actively pursuing federal grants, monitoring federal legislation, and participating in workforce investment boards have become new and important roles for the community college president.

Charitable Donations: The President as Fundraiser

Unlike many of their four-year counterparts, community colleges are playing catch-up when it comes to private giving. Historically, many two-year college leaders believed that fundraising was not the domain of the public community college. An American Association of Community Colleges research brief reported that two-year college presidents currently spend only 9.5 and 8.7 percent of their time, respectively, on fundraising and legislative activities (Weisman and Vaughan, 2001). However, as Chapter Four of this volume points out, community college leaders can no longer ignore or pay little attention to fundraising. This is not a responsibility that can be assigned to someone else. Most presidents, if asked, will confide that they do not like asking for money or that they have not been adequately trained in the practice. Unfortunately, future budget instability means that presidents have little choice but to vigorously pursue private giving.

To be effective fundraisers, community college presidents must have a basic understanding of giving options as well as familiarity with instruments for giving, such as charitable remainder trusts, charitable gift annuities, and gifts of insurance, stock, or real property. They must work closely with the college's foundation, assist in the selection of foundation board members, and spend considerable time with the foundation board chair, ensuring that fundraising is aligned with institutional priorities. Presidents should also be comfortable with the assessment, cultivation, and completion of gift arrangements from donors.

The fundraising skills needed to carry out these responsibilities can be learned from organizations such as the Clements Group of Salt Lake City, the Council for Resource Development of Washington, D.C., and the Council for the Advancement and Support of Education, also based in Washington, D.C. Each of these organizations offers a wide array of workshops and consulting options. In addition, presidents can stay current with the fund development literature by reviewing publications such as the *Chronicle of Philanthropy*.

Campus Morale and Board Relationships: The President as Communicator

Community college presidents must make changes in fiscal policy and practice in order to anticipate or respond to rapid shifts in budget streams. Yet presidents must also be aware that some of these changes may cause negative fallout among campus constituents. If campus leaders do not acknowledge and address changes in institutional direction setting, staffing, or operational methodologies early in the budget development process, faculty and staff will experience stress that will lead to declining morale, anger, and frustration. Luckily, much of this can be avoided.

As the leader of the college, the president must possess the skills necessary to assist the institution in times of change. If employees are made aware in advance of a situation or change in approach, most will understand and perhaps even help the president share the information across campus and in the community. Employees generally understand the volatile nature of higher education finances. What employees do not understand and clearly do not appreciate is being kept in the dark or left out of the situation. Presidents should be mindful of this and address college employees immediately.

The president's communication role and responsibility to the board for fiscal matters must be absolute. The governing board must never be surprised by financial problems or changes in fiscal direction. With increasing calls for accountability by the community at large, students, parents, and state and federal governments, presidents and governing boards should be in lockstep on fiscal priorities and decision making. Historically, financial matters involving discussions between the governing board and the president have generally occurred at specific chronological junctures, including annual budget approvals, tuition and fee setting, monthly finance reports, and audits. However, the president can no longer allow these to be the only times in which the governing board is involved in the college's finances.

Community college presidents must understand the board's financial expectations and operating parameters, as well as their level of understanding of fiscal matters. Ideally, the president should establish regular planning retreats with the board, so as to have adequate time to explore, discuss, and develop targeted fiscal solutions to institutional initiatives and challenges. These retreats will require considerable advance work by the president and his or her administration and staff. Briefing papers and recommendations should reflect the board's priorities, and should be distributed to members well in advance of the meeting. The meeting should provide opportunities for each board member to learn about and understand the implications of financial decisions.

Summary

The significant decline in state funding in recent years has tremendous implications for both current and potential presidents as fiscal leaders. The nature of financial decision making has changed appreciably over the last decade, and presidents now must demonstrate a new and expanded set of skills. Creativity, stewardship, and entrepreneurialism are vital skills for today's fiscal leader. "The imperative of rapidly changing economic, demographic, and political conditions suggests the need for adaptability and diversity in education institutions and their leaders. The challenges of growing enrollments, increasing fiscal pressures, and added government oversight may alter the character and chief responsibilities of the American college president" (American Council on Education, 2002, p. 47).

Taken together, these new and expanded roles represent a marked departure from the traditional role of the community college president, which was primarily as an educator. Because they are required to spend more time and effort on fiscal leadership and planning than ever before, many presidents may become troubled by their inability to be as involved in the curricular operations of the college as they once were. Given the reduced state support, as well as the regularity and speed of state cuts, college leaders have little choice but to embrace this change in focus, work with their governing boards to set institutional direction, and ensure that quality personnel are in key positions in the organization to carry out that charge. Presidents must be unambiguous about the college budget and clearly communicate the board and institution's priorities to college constituents. Addy (1995) remarked a decade ago that an organization's financial plans are the clearest indication of its intentions for the future, suggesting that it will require great intestinal fortitude to address financial issues. She spoke even more strongly about the president's role in finances, stating that "for the foreseeable future, budgeting and financial decisions will dominate everything that we do, every decision that we make, and every argument in which we engage about those decisions" (p. 90). Her statement is even more powerful and poignant today.

George Vaughan (2003), a former community college president, recently declared: "The president must take the lead in putting words into action—connecting the budget to the mission in ways that, in many cases, have not been done before. Whatever the institution's financial situation, it must spend limited resources so that it can best serve a wide variety of students. The budget should not be the sole determinant of what programs are offered, how many classes are provided, which students are admitted. That will require difficult decisions" (p. B24). Vaughan challenges the community college president to look beyond the low-hanging fruit in fiscal matters in order to fulfill the primary purpose of service to students. Clearly, each institution, each district, each community is unique. Thus, there will be no silver-bullet solution to diminishing support for community colleges, only the recognition that the college and its community demand vigilance, innovation, vision, and action from its fiscal leader.

References

Addy, C. L. *The President's Journey: Issues and Ideas in the Community College.* Bolton, Mass.: Anker, 1995.

American Council on Education. *The American College President.* Washington, D.C.: American Council on Education, 2002.

American Council on Education. *Rewriting the Rules of the Game: State Funding, Accountability, and Autonomy in Public Higher Education.* Washington, D.C.: American Council on Education, 2004.

Bernthal, T. "Association Office Memorandum." Lansing: Michigan Community College Association, 2005.

Boehner, J. A., and McKeon, H. P. *The College Cost Crisis: A Congressional Analysis of College Costs and Implication for America's Higher Education System.* Washington, D.C.: Committee on Education and the Workforce and Committee on 21st Century Competitiveness, House of Representatives, 2003. http://edworkforce.house.gov/ issues/108th/education/highereducation/CollegeCostCrisisReport.pdf. Accessed Sept. 27, 2005.

Boehner, J. A., and McKeon, H. P. "Official Correspondence." Washington, D.C.: Committee on Education and the Workforce, House of Representatives, June 2004. http://www.aacrao.org/federal_relations/position/Letter_to_College_Presidents.pdf. Accessed Sept. 27, 2005.

Boswell, K. "Keeping America's Promise: A Discussion Guide for State and Community College Leaders." In K. Boswell and C. D. Wilson (eds.), *Keeping America's Promise: A Report on the Future of the Community College.* Denver: Education Commission of the States, 2004.

Covey, S. R. *Principle-Centered Leadership: Strategies for Personal and Professional Effectiveness.* Salt Lake City, Utah: Franklin Covey, 1992.

Evelyn, J. "Community Colleges at a Crossroads." *Chronicle of Higher Education,* 2004, 50(34), A27–28.

Granholm, J. "Executive Order No. 2005–3: Implementation of Expenditure Reductions Under Section 20 of Article V of the Michigan Constitution of 1963." Lansing, Mich.: Office of the Governor, 2005. http://www.michigan.gov/gov/0,1607,7-168-21975-110450-,00.html. Accessed June 23, 2005.

Katsinas, S. G., Palmer, J. C., and Tollefson, T. A. "State Funding for Community Colleges: A View from the Field." Denton: University of North Texas, Bill J. Priest Center for Community College Education, 2004.

McClenney, K. M. "Keeping America's Promises: Challenges for Community Colleges."
    In K. Boswell and C. D. Wilson (eds.), *Keeping America's Promise: A Report on the
    Future of the Community College*. Denver: Education Commission of the States, 2004.
National Center for Public Policy and Higher Education. "Responding to the Crisis in
    College Opportunity." San Jose, Calif.: National Center for Public Policy in Higher
    Education, 2004. http://www.highereducation.org/reports/crisis/crisis.pdf. Accessed
    Aug. 9, 2005.
Vaughan, G. B. "Redefining 'Open Access.'" *Chronicle of Higher Education,* 2003, *50*(15),
    B24.
Weisman, I. M., and Vaughan, G. B. *The Community College Presidency*. Washington,
    D.C.: American Association of Community Colleges, 2001.

DANIEL J. PHELAN *is president and CEO of Jackson Community College in
Jackson, Michigan.*

10

This chapter reviews recent literature on the external fiscal environment in which community colleges operate and on the ways community colleges adapt to changes in that environment.

Literature on Fiscal Support for Community Colleges

James C. Palmer

Literature on community college fiscal support covers two broad themes. One group of writings explores the external fiscal environment in which colleges operate, examining trends and state-by-state variations in revenue streams, emerging approaches to state support (such as performance-based funding), and the ways in which government funding influences institutional behavior. A second theme involves fiscal management in the institutions themselves. Writers in this group analyze administrative approaches to retrenchment, planning mechanisms that support fiscal decision making, college efforts to secure private financial support, and other institutional adaptations to diminished public subsidy. This chapter reviews literature in both categories, drawing on selected journal articles and ERIC documents that have been published since 1990. These writings provide insights into the types of fiscal support on which community colleges rely and different institutional initiatives to sustain fiscal viability. The literature also highlights gaps in our knowledge about fiscal support for community colleges and its impact on the community college mission. Most of the resources highlighted in this chapter are available through the ERIC database at http://www.eric.ed. gov, and many more can be accessed online or at a local college or university library.

External Fiscal Environment

The literature offers at least four perspectives on the external fiscal environment in which community colleges operate. One is descriptive, documenting revenue streams across the states. For example, the Education

Commission of the States (2000) detailed the percent distribution of revenues by state for 1999, revealing, among other findings, that state funding as a proportion of total fiscal support ranged across the states from 14 to 71 percent. This suggests a slightly lower reliance on state funds than was the case in 1989, when state appropriations ranged from 25 to 85 percent (Garrett, 1992). In a more recent analysis, Kenton, Schuh, Huba, and Shelley (2004) documented trade-offs between funding sources in their analysis of community college revenues in ten midwestern states. These writers drew on IPEDS data for 1990, 1995, and 2000, and distributed the states into four categories based on their respective reliance on state tax appropriations, tuition and fees, and local tax appropriations. Across the four groups, the mean percentage of revenue by source ranged from 22.1 to 41.8 percent for state tax revenues, 16.0 to 28.9 percent for tuition and fees, and 0.8 to 33.9 percent for local tax appropriations. According to Kenton, Schuh, Huba, and Shelley, the group with the highest reliance on state taxes enjoyed the greatest overall increase in inflation-adjusted revenues from 1990 to 2000, but states in all groups experienced real gains in community college revenues, demonstrating that "in states where the level of funding from one source is low (e.g., local appropriations), community colleges look to other sources to sustain their revenue streams" (p. 10).

A second perspective on the external fiscal environment is longitudinal and is found in the work of those who examine trends in revenue streams over time. Here too trade-offs between revenue sources become apparent, especially between tuition on the one hand and local, state, or federal tax appropriations on the other. In their analysis of revenues received by midwestern community colleges in 1990, 1995, and 2000, Kenton, Huba, Schuh, and Shelley (2005) determined that reductions in state revenues during the 1990s (especially during the economic downturn experienced in the first half of the decade) were met in most cases by increased tuition, and to a lesser extent, by increases in local tax appropriations. However, Watkins's national analysis (2000) of community college revenues from 1989 to 1994 suggests that the tendency to increase tuition in the face of declining state appropriations may also be countered by increases in restricted government gifts, grants, and contracts. He determined that when combined, federal, state, and local tax appropriations decreased by $96 per full-time equivalent (FTE) student between 1989 and 1994. However, an increase of $281 per FTE student in government grants and contracts more than made up for the loss. The growth in government grants and contracts was also documented by Merisotis and Wolanin (2000) in their analysis of revenue trends from 1980 through 1996. Thus, although total government support per student actually increased during the early 1990s, college discretion in how these revenues can be spent probably declined, because most government grants and contracts are restricted to specific purposes (Watkins, 2000).

A third perspective offered by the literature is strategic and is expressed in occasional descriptions of "comparator-based" or "performance-based" funding systems that tie at least some state appropriations to institutional improvement or performance rather than enrollment. Henry (2000) described the comparator-based approach, in which state funding for community colleges is determined partially through comparisons with the fiscal support received by benchmark colleges in other states. He noted that requests for state aid are made with the intent of bringing "institutions to the level of funding received by the comparator colleges" (p. 43), and—in the tradition of performance-based funding—additional "base-plus" monies are sometimes offered as incentives for colleges "to address specific areas of high interest to the state, such as distance learning, workforce development, or reduction of unnecessary program duplication between institutions" (p. 43). Looking at performance-based plans across the states, Burke (1997) and Mize (1999) detailed the types of indicators they employ, whereas Pfeiffer (1998), Seppanen (1998), Freeman (2000), and Harbour (2002) examined performance-based funding in (respectively) Florida, Washington, Tennessee, and North Carolina. These writings suggest that although the performance-based approach has great appeal to state policymakers, its implementation may be slowed by difficulties in specifying performance indicators that are appropriate for community colleges and in maintaining computerized information systems needed to collect and analyze requisite data.

A fourth, analytic perspective stems from the work of researchers who examine the relationship between institutional autonomy and fiscal dependence on the state. For example, Garrett (1993) concluded that "state systems funded by more than 50 percent of state funds tend to have centralized governance structures" that impose relatively stringent controls on the colleges; in contrast, state systems in which local governments contribute more than 25 percent of community college funding "tend to have decentralized governance structures" (pp. 12–13). However, Tollefson (1997) noted exceptions to this general tendency, arguing that "other political factors and traditions are more important determinants of state control of community colleges than the proportion of operating support provided by the state" (p. 4). In addition, Fonte (1993) determined that even if the state does exert influence over institutional autonomy, the impact of this influence is mixed. Drawing on a survey of community college presidents and the directors of state community college systems, he found that colleges in states with "low" levels of state fiscal control were stronger than colleges in states with "medium" or "high" levels of state control in their capacity to provide programs and services that are "of particular interest to local employers or to their employees in their role as workers" (p. 6). In contrast, the level of state fiscal control was not as strongly associated with college capacity to provide courses of interest to local residents, engage in community service, or enhance access (as measured by tuition rates, the provision of instruction at convenient times, and the coordination of programs with high schools).

Internal Fiscal Management

Building on the work of those who examine the impact of external funding structures on community college functions are writers who analyze institutional adaptations to changes in the fiscal environment. Although Alfred (1996) calls for radical change, urging community colleges to aggressively create new markets for their services if they are to survive economically, most authors describe more conventional adaptations. For example, Ellis, Drake, LaPoint, and Russell (1995) determined that declines in state appropriations led Texas community colleges to adopt formal recession and reduction-in-force policies. In addition, Kapraun and Heard (1994) found that community colleges in Arkansas responded to appropriation declines in the early 1990s "by raising tuition, increasing the number of part-time faculty, and seeking new sources of revenue" (p. 508). Similarly, Levin, Perkins, and Clowes (1992) determined that the Virginia community colleges met reduced state funding in the 1980s with tuition increases, larger student-faculty ratios, staff reductions, more part-time faculty members, and reduced expenditures for maintenance, instructional equipment, and library acquisitions. Summarizing institutional responses to funding declines, Campbell, Leverty, and Sayles (1996) noted that community colleges raise tuition, develop self-supporting contracted education programs with local businesses, hire more part-time faculty members, and experiment with distance-learning technology as a way of reducing instructional costs.

A key question is whether declining appropriations, particularly from the state, threaten the colleges' commitment to open access or otherwise alter the community college mission. Writers in the early 1990s noted that although college leaders usually tried to absorb state funding declines without program cuts or other steps that would directly limit enrollment, a rethinking of open access and the comprehensive curriculum might well be inevitable (Collins, Leitzel, Morgan, and Stalcup, 1994; Leitzel, Morgan, and Stalcup, 1993; Levin, Perkins, and Clowes, 1992). These fears seem to be borne out by Sheldon (2003), who noted that "fiscal contraction by the state" (p. 77) led to the elimination of 10,500 class sections in the California community colleges in 2002 and 2003, as well as significant reductions in support for student services. In addition, Sheldon examined evidence of the impact of fee increases imposed by the California community colleges in the early 1990s, arguing that they decreased enrollment, and in combination with program cutbacks at the state's public four-year colleges, may have led to declines in the number of students transferring to baccalaureate institutions. Her analysis, written at the peak of the most recent recession, emphasizes the vulnerability of community college students to tuition and fee increases and calls into question community colleges' capacity to buffer core instructional programs from the effects of periodic economic downturns.

In the face of this threat, other authors describe fiscal decision-making techniques for allocating scarce resources in ways that optimize the return on investment. Drawing on an analysis showing that instructional costs are positively correlated with the number of faculty members employed per student as well as "the percentage of total enrollment in agricultural, skilled trade, and health programs" (p. 487), Watkins (1998) argues that community college leaders should carefully determine the number of course offerings and the optimal class size for each program area through an analysis of enrollment projections, benchmark data from other institutions, and research into the relationship between class size and student learning. Turning to economics, Romano (2002) draws on consumer-choice theory to describe a cost-benefit framework for deciding among alternative spending priorities. He argues that although logical determinations of the point at which "additional costs . . . exceed additional benefits" (p. 2) are not the only factors that should drive fiscal decision making at community colleges, they can help college leaders avoid decisions that "reflect only short-run emotional considerations or political expediency" (p. 12). This emphasis on rational analysis is mirrored in the planning models offered by Tambrino (2001) and Dellow and Losinger (2004) as a way of allocating resources among competing programs. Both models employ enrollment and cost data to determine the college's fiscal priorities and avoid the pitfall of allocating monies incrementally from year to year without testing assumptions about program viability or need. These authors argue that by rationally analyzing college costs and priorities, community colleges can make the best of what they have, especially in difficult fiscal times. As Dellow and Losinger (2004) explain, "The major new source of funding may well be the reallocation of resources within our existing budgets" (p. 688).

Related adaptations to fiscal uncertainty are institutional attempts to secure private funding through development offices, college foundations, or both. General overviews of the fundraising process at community colleges are provided by Glass and Jackson (1998), Brumbach and Villadsen (2002), Hall (2002), and Milliron, de los Santos, and Browning (2003). All of these authors stress that fundraising should focus on priorities identified in the college's strategic plan and employ leveraging strategies that use government grants to secure additional funding from private sources. They also argue that fundraising efforts should build on college partnerships with businesses and other community organizations that have a stake in what the college does and are therefore more willing to invest in its future. In addition, the literature offers descriptions of the fundraising efforts at individual colleges (Haire and Dodson-Pennington, 2002; Whiston, 2002), as well as studies examining the organization and administration of college development offices and foundations across the nation (Keener, Carrier, and Meaders, 2002), administrator perceptions of the factors driving fundraising in North Carolina's community colleges (Jackson and Glass, 2000), and the inception and subsequent growth of a community college foundation (Jenkins and Glass, 1999).

A Future Research Agenda

The studies described in this chapter provide periodic overviews of revenue trends nationwide, descriptions of state efforts to tie funding to institutional performance, and investigations of the relationship between state funding structures and institutional autonomy. They also examine administrative reactions to funding decreases, methodologies for fiscal decision making in the wake of these declines, and college efforts to secure private funds.

However, a more complete understanding of community college finance will require further investigation into the relationship between how the colleges are funded and what they do. Fonte's hypothesis (1993) that state fiscal regulation in the early 1990s worked against college responsiveness to local businesses, as well as Sheldon's description (2003) of the deleterious effects of funding decreases on the community college transfer function in California, provides tentative insights into the possible impacts of funding on the community college mission. Further analyses of the funding-mission relationship will be needed if we are to fully understand the implications of shifting revenue streams that have left community colleges less reliant on state appropriations than in the past and more dependent on tuition, government grants, and private funds.

In addition, researchers will need to move from national overviews to studies that investigate financial support in individual states. National data mask considerable state variations—as well as institutional variations *within* states—that are the product of local histories and political nuances. Take, for example, data on local tax support.

Community colleges in Florida do not receive local taxes (Florida Department of Education, 2005), a legacy of the decision to rely primarily on state funding as a means of ensuring the "equal fiscal treatment" of districts with differing levels of personal income and property wealth (Summers, Honeyman, Wattenbarger, and Miller, 1995, p. 239). In contrast, local tax monies accounted for 40 percent of total community college revenues in Illinois in 2003–04, and the proportion of revenues coming from local taxes ranged from 10 to 61 percent across institutions in that state (Illinois Community College Board, 2005). Clearly, the diversity of community college funding scenarios across the states will require researchers to augment national overviews with investigations of resource dependency in state community college systems.

References

Alfred, R. L. "Competition for Limited Resources: Realities, Prospects, and Strategies." In D. S. Honeyman, J. L. Wattenbarger, and K. C. Westbrook (eds.), *A Struggle to Survive: Funding Higher Education in the Next Century.* Thousand Oaks, Calif.: Corwin Press, 1996.

Brumbach, M. A., and Villadsen, A. W. "At the Edge of Chaos: The Essentials of Resource Development for the Community's College." *Community College Journal of Research and Practice,* 2002, 26(1), 77–86.

Burke, J. C. *Performance-Funding Indicators: Concerns, Values, and Models for Two- and Four-Year Colleges and Universities.* Albany: State University of New York, Nelson A. Rockefeller Institute of Government, 1997. (ED 407 910)

Campbell, D. F., Leverty, L. H., and Sayles, K. "Funding for Community Colleges." In D. S. Honeyman, J. L. Wattenbarger, and K. C. Westbrook (eds.), *A Struggle to Survive: Funding Higher Education in the Next Century.* Thousand Oaks, Calif.: Corwin Press, 1996.

Collins, S. E., Leitzel, T. C., Morgan, S. D., and Stalcup, R. J. "Declining Revenues and Increasing Enrollments: Strategies for Coping." *Community College Journal of Research and Practice,* 1994, *18*(1), 33–42.

Dellow, D. A., and Losinger, R. "A Management Tool for Reallocating College Resources." *Community College Journal of Research and Practice,* 2004, *28*(8), 677–688.

Education Commission of the States. *State Funding for Community Colleges: A 50-State Survey.* Denver, Colo.: Education Commission of the States, 2000. (ED 449 863)

Ellis, M., Drake, W., LaPoint, P., and Russell, K. "Retrenchment Policies in Public 2-Year Community Colleges in the State of Texas." *Community College Journal of Research and Practice,* 1995, *19*(6), 537–548.

Florida Department of Education. "The Fact Book: Report for the Florida Community College System." Tallahassee: Florida Department of Education, 2005. http://www.firn.edu/doe/arm/cctcmis/pubs/factbook/fb2005/factbk05.pdf. Accessed July 3, 2005.

Fonte, R. W. "The Impact of State Financing and Regulation on the Local Orientation of Community Colleges." *Community College Review,* 1993, *21*(1), 4–15.

Freeman, M. S. "The Experience of Performance Funding on Higher Education at the Campus Level in the Past 20 Years." Unpublished doctoral dissertation, University of Tennessee at Knoxville, 2000. (ED 466 845)

Garrett, R. L. *A Correlation Study of Selected Characteristics of States and State Community College Systems.* Florence, S.C.: Florence-Darlington Technical College, 1992. (ED 344 623)

Garrett, R. L. "A Profile of State Community College System Characteristics and Their Relationship to Degrees of Centralization." *Community College Review,* 1993, *20*(5), 6–15.

Glass, J. C., Jr., and Jackson, K. L. "Integrating Resource Development and Institutional Planning." *Community College Journal of Research and Practice,* 1998, *22*(8), 715–740.

Haire, C. M., and Dodson-Pennington, L. S. "Taking the Road Less Traveled: A Journey in Collaborative Resource Development." *Community College Journal of Research and Practice,* 2002, *26*(1), 61–75.

Hall, M. R. "Building on Relationships: A Fundraising Approach for Community Colleges." *Community College Journal of Research and Practice,* 2002, *26*(1), 47–60.

Harbour, C. P. "The Legislative Evolution of Performance Funding in the North Carolina Community College System." *Community College Review,* 2002, *29*(4), 28–49.

Henry, T. C. "From Theory to Practice: Implementing a State-Level Comparator-Based Funding Request and Allocation Model." *Community College Review,* 2000, *28*(3), 37–56.

Illinois Community College Board. "Data and Characteristics of the Illinois Community College Board." Springfield: Illinois Community College Board, 2005. http://www.iccb.state.il.us/HTML/pdf/reports/databook2005.pdf. Accessed July 31, 2005.

Jackson, K. L., and Glass, J. C., Jr. "Emerging Trends and Critical Issues Affecting Private Fund-Raising Among Community Colleges." *Community College Journal of Research and Practice,* 2000, *24*(9), 729–744.

Jenkins, L. W., and Glass, J. C., Jr. "Inception, Growth, and Development of a Community College Foundation: Lessons to Be Learned." *Community College Journal of Research and Practice,* 1999, *23*(6), 593–612.

Kapraun, E. D., and Heard, D. A. "Assessing the Financial and Institutional Concerns of Arkansas Community and Technical Colleges: A Model Approach." *Community College Journal of Research and Practice,* 1994, *18*(5), 499–509.

Keener, B. J., Carrier, S. M., and Meaders, S. J. "Resource Development in Community Colleges: A National Overview." *Community College Journal of Research and Practice,* 2002, *26*(1), 7–23.

Kenton, C. P., Huba, M. E., Schuh, J. H., and Shelley, M. C. "Financing Community Colleges: A Longitudinal Study of 11 States." *Community College Journal of Research and Practice,* 2005, *29*(2), 109–122.

Kenton, C. P., Schuh, J. H., Huba, M. E., and Shelley, M. C. "Funding Models of Community Colleges in 10 Midwest States." *Community College Review,* 2004, *32*(1), 1–17.

Leitzel, T. C., Morgan, S. D., and Stalcup, R. J. "Declining Revenues, Increasing Enrollments, and the Open Door." *Community College Journal of Research and Practice,* 1993, *17*(6), 489–495.

Levin, B. H., Perkins, J. R., and Clowes, D. A. "Changing Times, Changing Mission?" Paper presented at the annual conference of the Southeastern Association for Community College Research, Orlando, Fla., Aug. 1992. (ED 361 056)

Merisotis, J. P., and Wolanin, T. R. *Community College Financing: Strategies and Challenges.* New Expeditions: Charting the Second Century of Community Colleges. Issues paper no. 5. Washington, D.C.: American Association of Community Colleges, 2000. (ED 439 737)

Milliron, M. D., de los Santos, G. E., and Browning, B. (eds.). *Successful Approaches to Fundraising and Development.* New Directions for Community Colleges, no. 124. San Francisco: Jossey-Bass, 2003.

Mize, R. M. *Accountability Measures: A Comparison by Type and State.* Sacramento: Community College League of California, 1999. (ED 460 745)

Pfeiffer, J. J. "From Performance Reporting to Performance-Based Funding: Florida's Experiences in Workforce Development Performance Measurement." In J. R. Sanchez and F. S. Laanan (eds.), *Determining the Economic Benefits of Attending Community College.* New Directions for Community Colleges, no. 104. San Francisco: Jossey-Bass, 1998.

Romano, R. M. *Counting Beans at the Community College: An Exercise in Economic Rationality.* Binghamton, N.Y.: Institute for Community College Research, Broome Community College, 2002. (ED 469 660)

Seppanen, L. "Performance Funding on the Bleeding Edge: No Improvement, No Funding." Paper presented at the annual forum of the Association for Institutional Research, Minneapolis, May 1998. (ED 422 811)

Sheldon, C. Q. "ERIC Review: The Impact of Financial Crises on Access and Support Services in Community Colleges." *Community College Review,* 2003, *31*(2), 73–90.

Summers, S. R., Honeyman, D. S., Wattenbarger, J. L., and Miller, M. D. "An Examination of Supplantation and Redistribution Effects of Lottery Allocations to a Community College System." *Journal of Education Finance,* 1995, *21*(2), 236–253.

Tambrino, P. A. "Contribution Margin Budgeting." *Community College Journal of Research and Practice,* 2001, *14*(3), 34–40.

Tollefson, T. A. "Comparisons Between the State Share of Community College Operating Budgets and State Centralization of Control in Eleven State Community College Systems." Johnson City: East Tennessee State University, 1997. (ED 433 860)

Watkins, T. G. "Instructional Costs at Public Community Colleges." *Community College Journal of Research and Practice,* 1998, *22*(5), 479–490.

Watkins, T. G. "Public Community College Revenues, 1989–94." *Community College Journal of Research and Practice,* 2000, *24*(2), 95–106.

Whiston, K. "Rising Star Raises Success." *Community College Journal of Research and Practice,* 2002, *26*(10), 787–791.

JAMES C. PALMER *is professor of educational administration and foundations at Illinois State University.*

INDEX

Academic calendar, 62
Accountability, 51, 53–54, 82
Addy, C. L., 96
Adhocracy, 55–56
Advocates, 6, 7
Alfred, R. L., 102
Allocative efficiency, 36
American Association of Community Colleges, 26, 94
American Council on Education, 87, 89, 91, 92, 96
Americans for Tax Reform (ATR), 23–24
Antitax movement, 23–24
Architects, 70, 71
Arizona, 8t, 39, 91–92
Arkansas, 102
Ashe, J. L., 70
Assessment, 54, 62
Association of Community College Trustees, 94
Association of Governing Boards, 44, 46
ATR. *See* Americans for Tax Reform (ATR)
Autonomy, 101
Averianova, I. E., 3

Backman, D. L., 70
Bailey, T. R., 3
Balkan, E. M., 34
Bass, D., 44, 47
Batt, R., 49
Bernthal, T., 91
Betts, J. R., 40
Bittle, E. H., 70
Black institutions, 5
Boehner, J. A., 90, 94
Bond elections, 68–73, 81
Boosterism, 5
Boschee, F., 70
Boswell, K., 29, 91
Breneman, D. W., 15–16, 20, 33, 38
Brick, M., 6
Brint, S., 6–7
Brookhaven College: fundraising by, 47; workforce training at, 50–57
Browning, B., 103
Brumbach, M. A., 47, 49, 53, 56, 103

Budgets: operating efficiency of, 40; policy recommendations for, 40; strategic planning for, 80–84
Bureau of Justice Statistics, 22
Bureau of Labor Statistics, 26
Burke, J. C., 101
Bush, G. W., 22, 29, 88
Business partnerships, 47

California, 8, 9, 11, 39
Campbell, D. F., 102
Campus morale, 95–96
Capital markets, 37–38
Capital projects, 41
Carl D. Perkins Vocational and Technical Education Act, 93
Carlson, R. V., 70
Carrier, S. M., 20, 103
Case managers, 51, 55
Caterpillar, Inc.: and benefits of Think Big program, 64; and funding for Think Big program, 61; involvement of, in Think Big program, 62–63; and origin of Think Big program, 60–61; overview of, 59–60; and Think Big curriculum, 61–62; and Think Big evaluation, 63–64; and Think Big student recruitment, 62; and Think Big success, 64–65
Center for Community College Policy of the Education Commission of the States, 29
Charitable donations. *See* Fundraising
Charters, W. W., 11
Chicago, 69
Child care needs, 51
Child supervision, 5
Citizens' volunteer groups, 69–70, 71
Class sizes, 23, 80
Clements Group, 95
Clowes, D., 3, 102
College instructors, 52, 71
Collin County Community College District (CCCCD): enrollment in, 78; environmental scanning process at, 78–80; funding sources of, 78; overview of, 77–78; strategic planning at, 80–84

Collins, S. E., 102
Communal relationship, 44–45
Community colleges: coordinated fund-
   ing by, 20; early twentieth century
   decisions of, 7; mission of, 3, 104; sta-
   tus before 1940, 5, 6, 7
Community involvement, 44–45
Community partnerships, 46–47
Comparator-based funding systems,
   100–101
Compliance, 51, 53–54
Computer drives, 52
Connecticut, 68
Consumer-choice theory, 103
Contracts, 52–56
Conyers, J. G., 69, 72
Cooperative educational programs, 59
Coordinating boards. See State coordi-
   nating boards
Copa, G. H., 61
Corporate partnerships, 47, 62–63
Corrections facilities, 22
Cotton, M., 8
Council for Resource Development, 95
Council for the Advancement and Sup-
   port of Education, 44, 46, 95
Course offerings, 53
Covey, S. R., 93
Cray, E., 23
Creedy, J., 37
Crider, R. J., 69
Crime, 36
Critics, 6–7
Crosswait, B. N., 70, 71, 72
Cultural differences, 64–65
Curricula: experimentation with, 11; for
   Think Big program, 61–62
Curry, J. R., 82

Dallas County Community College Dis-
   trict, 44, 50, 92
Dalleck, M., 20
Databases, 54
de los Santos, G. E., 103
Dealer service technician programs,
   60–65
Decision-making techniques, 102–103
Dellow, D. A., 103
Development offices, 45–46
Developmental education, 28, 29
Didson-Pennington, L. S., 103
Distribution, of income, 34, 35
Diversity, 16
Division managers, 83–84

Documentation, 53–54
Dorweiler, P. J., 70
Dowd, A. C., 35
Drake, W., 102

Economy: and environmental scanning
   process, 78–80; good versus bad, 89;
   recent history of, 1
Education, benefits of, 36–37
Education Commission of the States, 39,
   99–100
Efficiency: case studies of, 39–40;
   overview of, 36; questions related to
   government grants and, 52; and student loans, 38; technical, 36, 39
Ehrenhalt, S. M., 23
Elections: for bonds, 81; president's role
   in, 89–90; for tax increases, 68–73
Elementary schools: and California's
   1921 legislation, 9; and equity, 35;
   mid-twentieth century spending on,
   22–23; partnerships with, 92–93
Ellis, M., 102
Ellison Miles Geotechnology Institute,
   50, 52–53
English as a Second Language classes, 37
Enrollment: in Collin County Community College District, 78; effects of
   recession on, 26; literature regarding,
   102–103; of lower versus middle- and
   upper-income students, 35; noncredit,
   26, 54; policy recommendations for,
   41; in Texas, 27
Environmental scanning process, 78–80
Equity: case studies of, 39–40; in early
   twentieth century funding, 14;
   overview of, 34; and state funding,
   67–68; and tax, 34–36; and tuition,
   35–36
Erwin, J., 3, 59
Evelyn, J., 88
Exchange relationship, 44–45
External effects, 36
External fiscal environment, 99–101

Fairness, 34
Federal grants. See Government-
   sponsored grants
Financial aid: and imperfect information,
   38; policy recommendations for,
   40–41
Fiscal dependence, 101
Fiscal Survey of the States, 1
Florida Department of Education, 104

Fonte, R. W., 101, 104
Food stamps, 79
Foote, J., 10
Foundations, 44, 46, 95
Francl, T., 69, 72
Free lunch programs, 79
Freeman, M. S., 101
Funding formula, 33
Fundraising: capacity for, 43; evolution of, 44; by foundations, 44; literature regarding, 103; in mid-twentieth century, 20; organized efforts for, 45–46; presidential leadership for, 45–46, 94–95; recent challenges of, 43; return on investment of, 46–47; scope of, 44–46

Garms, W. I., 38
Garrett, R. L., 100, 101
General obligation bonds, 81
Glass, J. C. Jr., 46, 103
Gott, P. L., 70, 72
Governing boards, 13, 92, 95–96
Government-sponsored grants: application for, 56–57; definition of, 49; management of, 51–52; questions pertinent to, 52–56; sources of, 93
Governors, 21
Graham, G. T., 70
Graham, L., 79
Granholm, J., 90
Grant, J. L., 35
Grants: current revenues for, 2t; management of, 49–50, 51–52; questions pertinent to, 52–56. See also specific types
Greene, K. V., 34
Greenleaf, W., 8
Grubb, W. N., 37

Hackett, D., 26
Haire, C. M., 103
Hall, M. R., 44–45, 46, 103
Hansen, W., 6
Harbour, C. P., 101
Hardin, T. L., 10
Hartley, R., 12
Health care: and environmental scanning process, 79; mid-twentieth century spending on, 21–22
Heard, D. A., 102
Hebel, S., 27
Hedgepeth, V., 7
Heffler, S., 21

Henry, J. M., 71, 72, 101
Herbkersman, N., 46
Herman, J. J., 70
Herz, D., 25, 26
Hibbert-Jones, K., 46
High schools. See Secondary schools
Higher Education Act, 5, 94
Hill, I., 85
Hipple, S., 25, 26
Historical records, 7–8
Historically black institutions, 5
Holt, C., 3, 67, 70, 72
Home foreclosures, 79
Honeyman, D. S., 104
Hovey, H. A., 22, 27
Huang, Y. H., 44
Huba, M. E., 67, 100
Huckabee, M., 22
Hurt, H. W., 8

Ibrahim, M. M., 82
Ideological polarization, 15–16
Illinois, 10
Illinois Central College (ICC): and benefits of Think Big program, 64; and Caterpillar's involvement in Think Big program, 62–63; and funding for Think Big program, 61; and origin of Think Big program, 60–61; overview of, 59–60; and Think Big curriculum, 61–62; and Think Big evaluation, 63–64; and Think Big student recruitment, 62; and Think Big success, 64–65
Illinois Community College Board, 104
Income distribution, 34, 35
Incremental budgeting system, 81–82
Indigent health care, 79
Information: about companies, 57; imperfections in, 38; in mill levy elections, 70–71; in zero-sum budgeting process, 83
Information economy, 25, 26
Infrastructure, 55
Instructional costs, 80
Interest groups, 10
Internal fiscal management, 102–103
Internships, 61–63
Iowa, 8t
IRATE (antitax group), 69
Israel, C., 3, 77

Jackson Community College, 92
Jackson, K. L., 45, 46, 103

Jenkins, D., 29
Jenkins, L. W., 46
Job loss, 51
Job training. *See* Workforce training
Job Training Partnership Act (1982), 26
Johnson, J. L., 21
Joliet Junior College, 10
Joyal, A., 7, 9
JPMorgan, 50
Junior College Act (1921), 9, 12
Junior College Act (1927), 14
"The Junior College Movement," 13
Junior colleges. *See* Community colleges

K–12 education. *See* Elementary schools;
    Secondary schools
Kaestle, C., 6
Kane, T. J., 37, 38, 40
Kansas, 11
Kapraun, E. D., 102
Karabel, J., 6–7
Katsinas, S., 3, 19, 21, 22, 25, 26, 27, 28,
    29, 92
Keener, B. J., 20, 45, 103
Kenton, C. P., 67, 100
Kerr, C., 20
Kiefer, D. W., 34
Kihl, B., 3, 77
King, D. B., 68
Kirp, D. L., 40
Koos, L., 7–8, 14

Lahti, R., 13
Laid-off workers, 26, 51
Land-grant institutions, 5
Lange, A. F., 9
Language barriers, 64–65
LaPoint, P., 102
Leadership training programs, 73
Learning communities, 16
Learning modules, 61–62
Leitzel, T. C., 102
Leslie, L. L., 3
Leverty, L. H., 102
Levin, B. H., 3, 102
Levine, D., 9
Levy increases, 68–73
Lincoln, A., 23
Literature, fiscal support, 99–104
Lobbyists, 89–90
Local tax. *See* Property tax; Sales tax
Lombardi, J., 1, 20
Losinger, R., 103
Louisiana, 10

Lower income students: enrollment of,
    35; imperfect information of, 38;
    tuition discounts for, 40

Manufacturing, 25, 53
Maricopa Community College District,
    92
Market failure, 36
Marketing techniques, 70, 91–93
Martinez, M. C., 28
Math programs, 23
Mathis, W. J., 23
Matthews, M., 63, 64
McClenney, K. M., 88
McFarland, L. L., 40
McGee, E. A., 45, 53
McKeon, H. P., 24, 90, 94
McPherson, M., 15
Meaders, S. J., 20, 103
Media, 70–71
Medicaid, 21–22
Mellor, E., 25, 26
Mentors, 63
Merisotis, J. P., 1
Merit-based financial aid, 41
Michigan, 11, 88, 90–91
Middle-income students, 35
Mill levy elections, 68–73
Miller, M., 3, 67, 104
Milliron, M., 87–88, 103
Minnesota, 28
Minnesota State Colleges and Universi-
    ties, 28
Missouri, 11
Mitchell, H. W. Jr., 70, 72
Mize, R. M., 101
Morale, 95–96
Morgan, S. D., 102
Mortensen, T. A., 24

Nardone, T., 25, 26
National Association of State Budget
    Officers, 1, 21, 22
National Center for Education Statistics,
    35
National Center for Public Policy and
    Higher Education, 88
National Governors Association, 1, 21,
    22
Nebraska, 14
Neighborhood effects, 36
Nelson, S. C., 15–16, 20, 33, 38
New federalism, 23
New York, 39–40

No Child Left Behind Act (NCLB), 23
Noncredit enrollments, 26, 54
Norquist, G., 23–24
North Carolina, 39, 40

Ogilvie, R., 20
Ohio, 10, 11–12
Ohio College Association, 12
Oklahoma, 8t
Open access: factors that limit, 88–89; prior to 1940, 7–9; reexamination of, 3–4
Open hearings, 83–84
Operating efficiency, 39–40
Osterman, P., 49

Palmer, J., 3, 22, 25, 27, 28, 29, 43, 92, 99
Palomar College Foundation, 46
Palomar Community College District, 46
Pear, R., 22
Pedersen, R., 1, 5
Pell grants: and antitax movement, 23–24; cost-coverage of, 20; rates of, 35
Pensoneau, T., 20
Performance-based finding systems, 100–101
Perkins, J. R., 3, 102
Pfeiffer, J. J., 101
Phelan, D., 3, 87
Phelan, J. F., 44
Physical science, 62
Planning retreats, 96
Political figures, 69
Political skills, 89–90
Poll watchers, 70
Portfolios, 54
Postgraduate programs, 11
Prall, C. E., 7, 8
Presidents, community college: as advocates, 93–94; and campus morale, 95–96; challenges of, 77, 87; as defenders of tuition, 90–91; as fundraisers, 94–95; and fundraising, 45–46; as lobbyists, 89–90; and mill levy elections, 69, 70; skills required of, 87–88, 96; as spokespeople, 91–93; tasks of, 87; and workforce training requests, 56
Priest, B. J., 20
Private benefits model, 23–24
Proctor, R. A., 82
Proctor, W. M., 9

Program evaluation, 63–64
Progressive tax structures, 34
Property tax, 34–35; availability of, 91–92; current funding from, 67; and equity issues, 67–68; levy increases in, 68–73
Proposition 13 (California), 1, 23
Provosts, 83–84
Public good, 36–37, 91
Public policy: guiding economic principles for, 33–34; recommendations for, 40–41; and tuition prior to 1940, 9; and view of funding, 5–6. See also State legislatures
Public subsidies: and efficiency, 36; and imperfect information, 38; and spillovers, 36–37; unequal distribution of, 6; value judgments underlying, 34. See also specific types
Puyear, D. E., 67
Puzey, J., 72

Rafai, S., 83
Reagan, R., 20, 23–24
Recessions: effects of, 1, 19; methods for dealing with, 25–26; number of, 25
Recruitment, student, 62
Regressive taxes, 34, 41
Reid, B. L., 44
Relationship building, 91–93
Remedial education, 37
Retirement, 88
Revenue bonds, 81
Richardson, R. C., 3
Rising Star program, 44
Romanik, D. G., 70
Romano, R., 3, 33, 34, 37, 38–39, 41, 103
Ross, V. J., 72
Rouse, C. E., 37, 39
Rural areas, 47, 73
Russell, K., 102
Ryan, J., 3, 43

Salaries, 62–63
Sales tax, 34; current funding from, 67; levy increases in, 68–73
Sayles, K., 102
Schapiro, M., 15
School boards, 11, 12
School superintendents, 92–93
Schuh, J. H., 67, 100
Science programs, 23, 62
Secondary schools: and California's 1921

legislation, 9; curricular initiatives of, 11; and equity, 35; mid-twentieth century spending on, 22–23; partnerships with, 92–93

Security screenings, 52

Semiconductor chip manufacturing, 53

Seminars, 55

Senate Journal of the Twenty-First Legislature, 12

Seppanen, L., 101

Sewender, H. J., 26

Shek, K., 26

Sheldon, C. Q., 102, 104

Shelley, M. C., 67, 100

Short, J. M., 28

Six-year high schools, 11

Skills Development Fund grant, 50

Social benefits, of education, 6, 36–37

Soft skills, 53

Special education programs, 23

Spillovers, 36–37

Stalcup, R. J., 102

Standards-based education, 23

State appropriations: in California history, 9; current revenues for, 2t; effect of reduction in, 27–28; literature regarding, 102–103; in mid-twentieth century, 20–23; and tasks of state legislatures, 10

State budget: challenges of, 1, 2t; effects of recession on, 25; implications of, 27–29

State coordinating boards: advocacy strength of, 21; formalization of, 20; in mill levy elections, 69

State Higher Education Executive Officers, 67

State legislatures: early twentieth century restrictions used by, 11–13; in mid-twentieth century, 20–23; priorities of, 19; recognition of community colleges by, 10–11; responsibilities of, 15; self-interest of, 10; tasks of, 10. See also Public policy

State of the District address, 85

State universities: early opposition from, 13–14; policy recommendations for, 41

Stipends, 80

Strategic planning, 46, 80–84

Structural state budget deficit, 22

Student loans, 28, 38

Student recruitment, 62

Subcontracting, 53–54

Subrecipients, 54

Subsidies. See Public subsidies

Summers, S. R., 104

Supervision, of children, 5

Surratt, J. E., 69

Tambrino, P. A., 103

TANF. See Temporary Assistance for Needy Families (TANF)

Tax: early twentieth century policies regarding, 7, 13, 14; effects of appropriations reductions on, 27–28; and equity, 34–36; for funding Texas schools, 78; literature related to, 100; movement against, 23–24. See also specific types

Taylor, A., 83

Taylor, K., 69

Technical efficiency, 36, 39

Temporary Assistance for Needy Families (TANF), 51, 54, 79

Term limits movement, 23

Texas, 8t, 27, 85

Texas Association of Community Colleges, 27, 78

Texas Workforce Commission, 79

Think Big program: benefits of, 64; dealership involvement in, 62–63; evaluation of, 63–64; funding for, 61; origin of, 60–61; overview of, 59–60; student recruitment for, 62; success of, 64–65

Third-party expenditures, 80–81

Thompson, J., 21

Tidal Wave II, 26

Tillery, D., 19

Tolerance, 36

Tollefson, T. A., 22, 27, 28, 29, 92

Trade Adjustment Act, 51

Transfers, 73

Trustees, 46, 69

Tuition: and antitax movement, 24–25; current revenues for, 2t; disadvantages of using, 33; in early twentieth century, 7–9, 13, 14; effects of recession on, 25; effects of reduced appropriations on, 27–28; and equity, 35–36; policy recommendations for, 40; presidents as defenders of, 90–91; public's recommendation regarding, 92; and reauthorization of Higher Education Act, 5; recent increases in, 88–89; and spillovers, 37

Turner, E. C., 10

Unemployment, 26, 79
University extension center, 11
University of Wyoming, 13, 15
Upper-income students, 35
Upward extension programs, 11
U.S. Bureau of Education, 8
U.S. Department of Education, 35
Utah, 10

Vaughan, G. B., 3, 94, 97
Vice presidents, 83–84
Villadsen, A. W., 47, 56, 103
Virginia, 102

Warren, E., 23
Washington, 10, 12–13
Watkins, T. G., 1, 100, 103
Wattenbarger, J. L., 19, 104
Weisbrod, B., 6
Weisman, I. M., 94
Wellman, J. V., 22
Wenrich, J. W., 44
Wheeler, G., 69
Whiston, K., 44, 103
WIA. *See* Workforce Investment Act (WIA)

Wildavsky, A., 83
Williams, J. J., 83
Winchell, K., 13
Winston, G., 15
Wise, G. L., 70
Wolanin, T. R., 1, 100
Wolff, S. J., 61
Wood, W. C., 9
Workforce Investment Act (WIA), 51, 54
Workforce training: at Brookhaven College, 50–57; common requests for, 49, 55–56; community colleges obligation to, 59; grant management for, 51–52; predicted decline in funding for, 28; questions to ask before applying for grant for, 52–56. *See also specific programs*
Wright, J., 60, 63
Wyoming, 13–14
Wyoming Community College Records Manual, 13

Zero-sum budgeting, 82–84
Zook, G. F., 12, 14

Back Issue/Subscription Order Form

Copy or detach and send to:
Jossey-Bass, A Wiley Imprint, 989 Market Street, San Francisco CA 94103-1741

Call or fax toll-free: Phone 888-378-2537 6:30AM – 3PM PST; Fax 888-481-2665

Back Issues: Please send me the following issues at $29 each
(Important: please include ISBN number for each issue.)

_____

_____

_____

$ _____   Total for single issues

$ _____   SHIPPING CHARGES: SURFACE   Domestic   Canadian

	Domestic	Canadian
First Item	$5.00	$6.00
Each Add'l Item	$3.00	$1.50

For next-day and second-day delivery rates, call the number listed above.

Subscriptions   Please __ start __ renew my subscription to *New Directions for Community Colleges* for the year 2____at the following rate:

U.S.	__ Individual $80	__ Institutional $180
Canada	__ Individual $80	__ Institutional $220
All Others	__ Individual $104	__ Institutional $254

Online subscriptions are available too!

**For more information about online subscriptions visit
www.interscience.wiley.com**

$ _____   Total single issues and subscriptions (Add appropriate sales tax for your state for single issue orders. No sales tax for U.S. subscriptions. Canadian residents, add GST for subscriptions and single issues.)

__Payment enclosed (U.S. check or money order only)
__VISA __ MC __ AmEx __ # _____Exp. Date _____

Signature _____ Day Phone _____
__ Bill Me (U.S. institutional orders only. Purchase order required.)

Purchase order # _____
      Federal Tax ID13559302   **GST 89102 8052**

Name _____

Address _____

_____

Phone _____ E-mail _____

For more information about Jossey-Bass, visit our Web site at www.josseybass.com

OTHER TITLES AVAILABLE IN THE
NEW DIRECTIONS FOR COMMUNITY COLLEGES SERIES
Arthur M. Cohen, Editor-in-Chief
Florence B. Brawer, Associate Editor

CC131 **Community College Student Affairs: What Really Matters**
Steven R. Helfgot, Marguerite M. Culp
Uses the results of a national survey to identify the major challenges and
opportunities for student affairs practitioners in community colleges,
and describes the most effective strategies for meeting challenges. Chapters
discuss core values, cultures of evidence, faculty partnerships, career
counseling, and support for underrepresented populations, plus assessment
tools and best practices in student affairs.
ISBN: 0-7879-8332-2

CC130 **Critical Thinking: Unfinished Business**
Christine M. McMahon
With a few exceptions, critical thinking is not being effectively taught nor
even correctly understood in higher education. This volume advocates for
professional development in critical thinking to engage all members of the
campus community. It presents blueprints for such development, plus
practical case studies from campuses already doing it. Also covers classroom
assignments, solutions to resistance, and program assessment.
ISBN: 0-7879-8185-0

CC129 **Responding to the Challenges of Developmental Education**
Carol A. Kozeracki
Approximately 40 percent of incoming community college students enroll in
developmental math, English, or reading courses. Despite the availability of
popular models for teaching these classes, community colleges continue to
struggle with effectively educating underprepared students, who have a wide
variety of backgrounds. This volume discusses the dangers of isolating
developmental education from the broader college; provides examples of
successful programs; offers recommendations adaptable to different
campuses; and identifies areas for future research.
ISBN: 0-7879-8050-1

CC128 **From Distance Education to E-Learning: Lessons Along the Way**
Beverly L. Bower, Kimberly P. Hardy
Correspondence, telecourses, and now e-learning: distance education
continues to grow and change. This volume's authors examine what
community colleges must do to make distance education successful, including
meeting technology challenges, containing costs, developing campuswide
systems, teaching effectively, balancing faculty workloads, managing student
services, and redesigning courses for online learning. Includes case studies
from colleges, plus state and regional policy perspectives.
ISBN: 0-7879-7927-9

CC127 **Serving Minority Populations**
Berta Vigil Laden
Focuses on how colleges with emerging majority enrollments of African
American, Hispanic, American Indian, Asian American and Pacific Islander,
and other ethnically diverse students are responding to the needs—
academic, financial, and cultural—of their increasingly diverse student
populations. Discusses partnerships with universities, businesses,

foundations, and professional associations that can increase access, retention, and overall academic success for students of color. Covers best practices from Minority-Serving Institutions, and offers examples for mainstream community colleges.
ISBN: 0-7879-7790-X

CC126 **Developing and Implementing Assessment of Student Learning Outcomes**
Andreea M. Serban, Jack Friedlander
Colleges are under increasing pressure to produce evidence of student learning, but most assessment research focuses on four-year colleges. This volume is designed for practitioners looking for models that community colleges can apply to measuring student learning outcomes at the classroom, course, program, and institutional levels to satisfy legislative and accreditation requirements.
ISBN: 0-7879-7687-3

CC125 **Legal Issues in the Community College**
Robert C. Cloud
Community colleges must be prepared for lawsuits, federal statutes, court rulings, union negotiations, and other legal issues that could affect institutional stability and effectiveness. This volume provides leaders with information about board relations, tenure and employment, student rights and safety, disability law, risk management, copyright and technology issues, and more.
ISBN: 0-7879-7482-X

CC124 **Successful Approaches to Fundraising and Development**
Mark David Milliron, Gerardo E. de los Santos, Boo Browning
This volume outlines how community colleges can tap into financial support from the private sector, as four-year institutions have been doing. Chapter authors discuss building community college foundations, cultivating relationships with the local community, generating new sources of revenue, fundraising from alumni, and the roles of boards, presidents, and trustees.
ISBN: 0-7879-7283-5

CC123 **Help Wanted: Preparing Community College Leaders in a New Century**
William E. Piland, David B. Wolf
This issue brings together various thoughtful perspectives on the nature of leading community colleges over the foreseeable future. Authors offer suggestions for specific programmatic actions that community colleges themselves can take to provide the quantity, quality, specializations, and diversity of leaders that are needed.
ISBN: 0-7879-7248-7

CC122 **Classification Systems for Two-Year Colleges**
Alexander C. McCormick, Rebecca D. Cox
This critically important volume advances the conversation among researchers and practitioners about possible approaches to classifying two-year colleges. After an introduction to the history, purpose, practice, and pitfalls of classifying colleges and universities, five different classification schemes are presented, followed by commentary by knowledgable respondents representing potential users of a classification system: community college associations, institutional leaders, and researchers. The final chapter applies the five proposed schemes to a sample of colleges for purposes of illustration.
ISBN: 0-7879-7171-5

CC121 **The Role of the Community College in Teacher Education**
Barbara K. Townsend, Jan M. Ignash
Illustrates the extent to which community colleges have become major players in teacher education, not only in the traditional way of providing the first two years of an undergraduate degree in teacher education but in more controversial ways such as offering associate and baccalaureate degrees in teacher education and providing alternative certification programs.
ISBN: 0-7879-6868-4

CC120 **Enhancing Community Colleges Through Professional Development**
Gordon E. Watts
Offers a much needed perspective on the expanding role of professional development in community colleges. Chapter authors provide descriptions of how their institutions have addressed issues through professional development, created institutional change, developed new delivery systems for professional development, reached beyond development just for faculty, and found new uses for traditional development activities.
ISBN: 0-7879-6330-5

CC119 **Developing Successful Partnerships with Business and the Community**
Mary S. Spangler
Demonstrates that there are many different approaches to community colleges' partnering with the private sector and that when partners are actively engaged in tailoring education, training, and learning to their students, everyone is the beneficiary.
ISBN: 0-7879-6321-9

CC118 **Community College Faculty: Characteristics, Practices, and Challenges**
Charles Outcalt
Offers multiple perspectives on the ways community college faculty fulfill their complex professional roles. With data from national surveys, this volume provides an overview of community college faculty, looks at their primary teaching responsibility, and examines particular groups of instructors, including part-timers, women, and people of color.
ISBN: 0-7879-6328-3

CC117 **Next Steps for the Community College**
Trudy H. Bers, Harriott D. Calhoun
Provides an overview of relevant literature and practice covering major community college topics: transfer rates, vocational education, remedial and developmental education, English as a second language education, assessment of student learning, student services, faculty and staff, and governance and policy. Includes a chapter discussing the categories, types, and purposes of literature about community colleges and the major publications germane to community college practitioners and scholars.
ISBN: 0-7879-6289-9

CC116 **The Community College Role in Welfare to Work**
C. David Lisman
Provides examples of effective programs including a job placement program meeting the needs of rural welfare recipients, short-term and advanced levels of technical training, a call center program for customer service job training,

beneficial postsecondary training, collaborative programs for long-term family economic self-sufficiency, and a family-based approach recognizing the needs of welfare recipients and their families.
ISBN: 0-7879-5781-X

CC115   **The New Vocationalism in Community Colleges**
Debra D. Bragg
Analyzes the role of community college leaders in developing programs, successful partnerships and collaboration with communities, work-based learning, changes in perception of terminal education and transfer education, changing instructional practices for changing student populations and the integration of vocational education into the broader agenda of American higher education.
ISBN: 0-7879-5780-1

CC114   **Transfer Students: Trends and Issues**
Frankie Santos Laanan
Evaluates recent research and policy discussions surrounding transfer students, and summarizes three broad themes in transfer policy: research, student and academic issues, and institutional factors. Argues that institutions are in a strategic position to provide students with programs for rigorous academic training as well as opportunities to participate in formal articulation agreements with senior institutions.
ISBN: 0-7879-5779-8

CC113   **Systems for Offering Concurrent Enrollment at High Schools and Community Colleges**
Piedad F. Robertson, Brian G. Chapman, Fred Gaskin
Offers approaches to creating valuable programs, detailing all the components necessary for the success and credibility of concurrent enrollment. Focuses on the faculty liaisons from appropriate disciplines that provide the framework for an ever-improving program.
ISBN: 0-7879-5758-5

CC112   **Beyond Access: Methods and Models for Increasing Retention and Learning Among Minority Students**
Steven R. Aragon
Presents practical models, alternative approaches and new strategies for creating effective cross-cultural courses that foster higher retention and learning success for minority students. Argues that educational programs must now develop a broader curriculum that includes multicultural and multi-linguistic information.
ISBN: 0-7879-5429-2

CC111   **How Community Colleges Can Create Productive Collaborations with Local Schools**
James C. Palmer
Details ways that community colleges and high schools can work together to help students navigate the difficult passage from secondary to higher education. Provides detailed case studies of actual collaborations between specific community colleges and high school districts, discuss legal problems that can arise when high school students enroll in community colleges, and more.
ISBN: 0-7879-5428-4

NEW DIRECTIONS FOR COMMUNITY COLLEGES
IS NOW AVAILABLE ONLINE AT WILEY INTERSCIENCE

What is Wiley InterScience?

Wiley InterScience is the dynamic online content service from John Wiley & Sons delivering the full text of over 300 leading scientific, technical, medical, and professional journals, plus major reference works, the acclaimed *Current Protocols* laboratory manuals, and even the full text of select Wiley print books online.

What are some special features of Wiley InterScience?

Wiley InterScience Alerts is a service that delivers table of contents via e-mail for any journal available on Wiley InterScience as soon as a new issue is published online.
Early View is Wiley's exclusive service presenting individual articles online as soon as they are ready, even before the release of the compiled print issue. These articles are complete, peer-reviewed, and citable.
CrossRef is the innovative multi-publisher reference linking system enabling readers to move seamlessly from a reference in a journal article to the cited publication, typically located on a different server and published by a different publisher.

How can I access Wiley InterScience?

Visit http://www.interscience.wiley.com

Guest Users can browse Wiley InterScience for unrestricted access to journal Tables of Contents and Article Abstracts, or use the powerful search engine.
Registered Users are provided with a *Personal Home Page* to store and manage customized alerts, searches, and links to favorite journals and articles. Additionally, Registered Users can view free Online Sample Issues and preview selected material from major reference works.
Licensed Customers are entitled to access full-text journal articles in PDF, with select journals also offering full-text HTML.

How do I become an Authorized User?

Authorized Users are individuals authorized by a paying Customer to have access to the journals in Wiley InterScience. For example, a university that subscribes to Wiley journals is considered to be the Customer. Faculty, staff and students authorized by the university to have access to those journals in Wiley InterScience are Authorized Users. Users should contact their Library for information on which Wiley journals they have access to in Wiley InterScience.

ASK YOUR INSTITUTION ABOUT WILEY INTERSCIENCE TODAY!

United States Postal Service

Statement of Ownership, Management, and Circulation

1. Publication Title	2. Publication Number	3. Filing Date
New Directions For Community Colleges	0 1 1 9 4 – 3 0 8 1	10/1/05

4. Issue Frequency	5. Number of Issues Published Annually	6. Annual Subscription Price
Quarterly	4	$180.00

7. Complete Mailing Address of Known Office of Publication (Not printer) (Street, city, county, state, and ZIP+4)

Wiley Subscription Services, Inc. at Jossey-Bass, 989 Market Street, San Francisco, CA 94103

Contact Person
Joe Schuman
Telephone
(415) 782-3232

8. Complete Mailing Address of Headquarters or General Business Office of Publisher (Not printer)

Wiley Subscription Services, Inc. 111 River Street, Hoboken, NJ 07030

9. Full Names and Complete Mailing Addresses of Publisher, Editor, and Managing Editor (Do not leave blank)

Publisher (Name and complete mailing address)

Wiley, San Francisco, 989 Market Street, San Francisco, CA 94103-1741

Editor (Name and complete mailing address)

Arthur M. Cohen, Eric Clearinghouse for Community Colleges, 3051 Moore Hall, Box 95121, Los Angeles, CA 90095-1521

Managing Editor (Name and complete mailing address)

None

10. Owner (Do not leave blank. If the publication is owned by a corporation, give the name and address of the corporation immediately followed by the names and addresses of all stockholders owning or holding 1 percent or more of the total amount of stock. If not owned by a corporation, give the names and addresses of the individual owners. If owned by a partnership or other unincorporated firm, give its name and address as well as those of each individual owner. If the publication is published by a nonprofit organization, give its name and address.)

Full Name	Complete Mailing Address
Wiley Subscription Services, Inc.	111 River Street, Hoboken, NJ 07030
(see attached list)	

11. Known Bondholders, Mortgagees, and Other Security Holders Owning or Holding 1 Percent or More of Total Amount of Bonds, Mortgages, or Other Securities. If none, check box. ☑ None

Full Name	Complete Mailing Address
None	

12. Tax Status (For completion by nonprofit organizations authorized to mail at nonprofit rates) (Check one)
The purpose, function, and nonprofit status of this organization and the exempt status for federal income tax purposes:
☐ Has Not Changed During Preceding 12 Months
☐ Has Changed During Preceding 12 Months (Publisher must submit explanation of change with this statement)

PS Form 3526, October 1999   (See Instructions on Reverse)

13. Publication Title	14. Issue Date for Circulation Data Below
New Directions For Community Colleges	Summer 2005

15.	Extent and Nature of Circulation	Average No. Copies Each Issue During Preceding 12 Months	No. Copies of Single Issue Published Nearest to Filing Date
a.	Total Number of Copies (Net press run)	1737	1702
b. Paid and/or Requested Circulation	(1) Paid/Requested Outside-County Mail Subscriptions Stated on Form 3541. (Include advertiser's proof and exchange copies)	724	713
	(2) Paid In-County Subscriptions Stated on Form 3541 (Include advertiser's proof and exchange copies)	0	0
	(3) Sales Through Dealers and Carriers, Street Vendors, Counter Sales, and Other Non-USPS Paid Distribution	0	0
	(4) Other Classes Mailed Through the USPS	0	0
c.	Total Paid and/or Requested Circulation [Sum of 15b. (1), (2),(3),and (4)]	724	713
d. Free Distribution by Mail (Samples, compliment ary, and other free)	(1) Outside-County as Stated on Form 3541	0	0
	(2) In-County as Stated on Form 3541	0	0
	(3) Other Classes Mailed Through the USPS	0	0
e.	Free Distribution Outside the Mail (Carriers or other means)	146	145
f.	Total Free Distribution (Sum of 15d. and 15e.)	146	145
g.	Total Distribution (Sum of 15c. and 15f)	870	858
h.	Copies not Distributed	867	844
i.	Total (Sum of 15g. and h.)	1637	1702
j.	Percent Paid and/or Requested Circulation (15c. divided by 15g. times 100)	83%	83%

16. Publication of Statement of Ownership
☑ Publication required. Will be printed in the Winter 2005 issue of this publication.   ☐ Publication not required.

17. Signature and Title of Editor, Publisher, Business Manager, or Owner

Susan E. Lewis, VP & Publisher - Periodicals   Date 10/01/05

I certify that all information furnished on this form is true and complete. I understand that anyone who furnishes false or misleading information on this form or who omits material or information requested on the form may be subject to criminal sanctions (including fines and imprisonment) and/or civil sanctions (including civil penalties).

Instructions to Publishers

1. Complete and file one copy of this form with your postmaster annually on or before October 1. Keep a copy of the completed form for your records.

2. In cases where the stockholder or security holder is a trustee, include in items 10 and 11 the name of the person or corporation for whom the trustee is acting. Also include the names and addresses of individuals who are stockholders who own or hold 1 percent or more of the total amount of bonds, mortgages, or other securities of the publishing corporation. In item 11, if none, check the box. Use blank sheets if more space is required.

3. Be sure to furnish all circulation information called for in item 15. Free circulation must be shown in items 15d, e, and f.

4. Item 15h., Copies not Distributed, must include (1) newsstand copies originally stated on Form 3541, and returned to the publisher, (2) estimated returns from news agents, and (3), copies for office use, leftovers, spoiled, and all other copies not distributed.

5. If the publication had Periodicals authorization as a general or requester publication, this Statement of Ownership, Management, and Circulation must be published; it must be printed in any issue in October or, if the publication is not published during October, the first issue printed after October.

6. In item 16, indicate the date of the issue in which this Statement of Ownership will be published.

7. Item 17 must be signed.

Failure to file or publish a statement of ownership may lead to suspension of Periodicals authorization.

PS Form 3526, October 1999 (Reverse)